Udder Confusion

An Alaska Homesteader's
True-Life Adventures

Elverda E. Lincoln

Publication Consultants
Since 1978

PO Box 221974 Anchorage, Alaska 99522-1974
books@publicationconsultants.com—www.publicationconsultants.com

ISBN 978-1-59433-113-8

Library of Congress Catalog Card Number: 2009936690

Manufactured in the United States of America.

Acknowledgments

I express my gratitude to Margaret Swensen and Paula A. Groundwater for their expertise, patience, and encouragement in helping me get *Udder Confusion* ready for publication.

To my granddaughter, Kristin Lincoln, I give special recognition for the artwork. Ersa Kelley's reading and proofing of the completed manuscript is appreciated. To our neighbors and friends, those who helped us over the tough times, and whose stories are part of ours, thank you. It's you who have made Udder Confusion the best part of our life.

Every word in this book is true, at least the way I remember it. Some things can't be told until the Statute of Limitations expires. Many good stories have been left out to protect my neighbors—and myself.

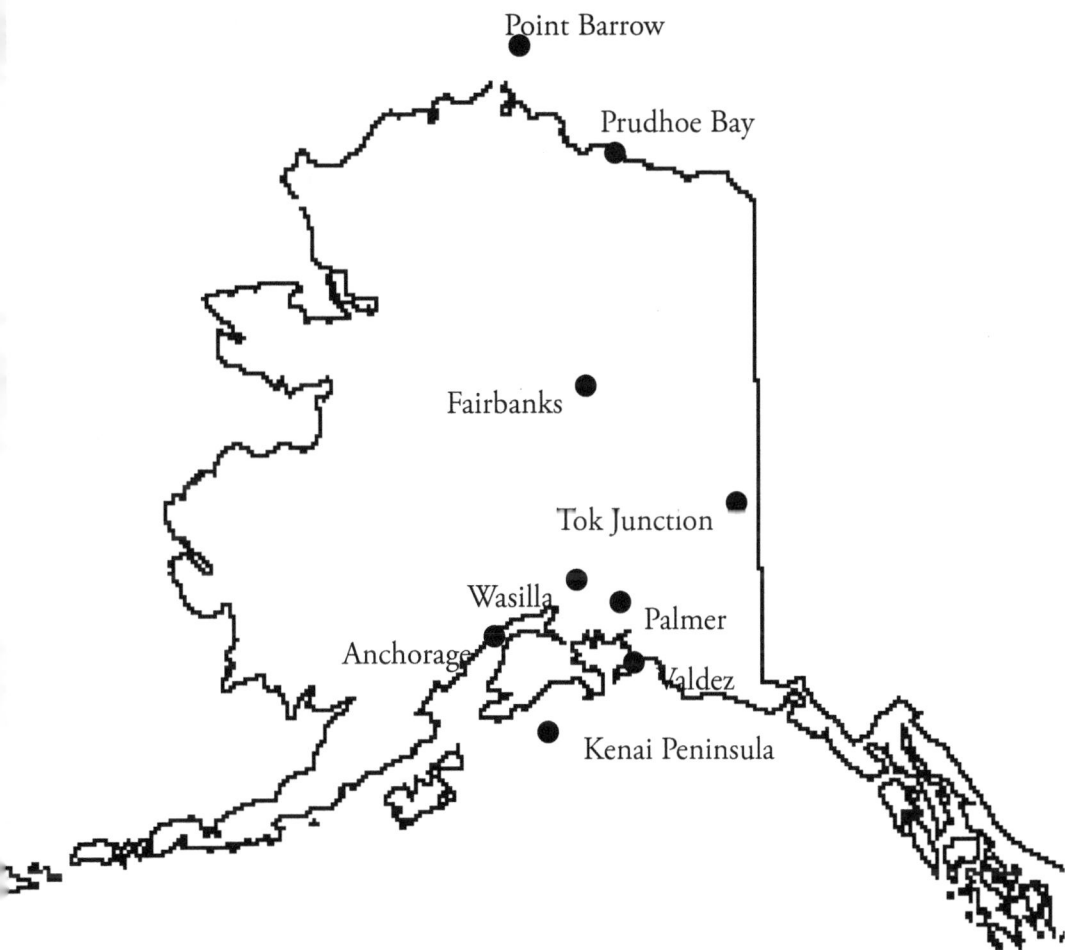

Point Barrow

Prudhoe Bay

Fairbanks

Tok Junction

Wasilla

Palmer

Anchorage

Valdez

Kenai Peninsula

Dedication

Dedicated to my husband, Bob, and my children Roger, Barbara, and Linda, who made this book possible.

Table of Contents

Barbara and Linda 13

Roger 15

Off to Alaska - 1950 17

First Summer 29

First Winter 37

The Fritzler Place 45

Udder Confusion 61

Udder Confusion Photo Album 91

Adam's Apple 129

Alaska Earthquake 131

Bears and Sawdust 135

Bill Collectors 137

A Boy's Summer 139

Bread Making...143

Dog Team 145

Fall, My Favorite Time 147

GI Schooling...149

Go to Hell...151

Kennedy's Mud hole...153

Kids 155

One Salmon 159

One Fish Again 161

Over the Hill...163

Sawmill Sourdough Style..165

Sourdough in Prison...167

The Bus Driver 169

Tooth and Tire 171

Lincoln Said...173

Rhubarb Wine 175

Neighbors and Friends 177

Gandy Dancing...179

Gardening and Harvesting 181

Roger's Enterprise...183

Plump Stump Sisters 185

Epilog 189

Barbara and Linda

A number of our parents' experiences happened when we were quite young. It was interesting and entertaining to read stories we've heard, laughed about, or discussed over the years. Many childhood memories were fondly brought back to us. Growing up on a homestead developed a self-sufficiency and work ethic which we've maintained over the years. Living on a homestead probably kept us out of trouble too. Even though life on a homestead involved hard work for us, there were also lots of fun and experiences that we wouldn't want to miss. We can't think of a better way to grow up, or a better place to grow up on, than a homestead.

Roger

When I read the manuscript, memories of my early years came flooding back. Many things my mother wrote about, I had long forgotten. Now that I'm married with a family of my own, I can identify with many challenges that my parents faced. Although times have changed, many problems are the same. Each generation thinks they've never had it so good, and, yet the succeeding generations look back and are thankful they never had it that hard. In 30 years, these times we're now living will be the good old days. In spite of the difficulties, I'm sure my parents feel they lived in the good old days.

Read and enjoy these stories. They're true. Laugh, weep, and share their times with them. Someday, you, too, will have lived in the good old days.

Off to Alaska—1950

We made the bold, startling announcement to our friends and relatives. We were going to begin a new life on the Kenai Peninsula in Alaska. When we announced our plans, a variety of reactions surfaced. Bob's sister, Roxie, shook her head, "Alaska, you guys must be crazy. As far as I am concerned, you might as well go to Russia!"

My father smugly responded to our announcement, "You'll be back. You can't get along without old Pop!"

A friend tearfully commented to us, "We'll probably never see you again!"

"You mean you're going to farm in Alaska?" my sister remarked. "What are you going to harvest, ice and snow?"

"Go ahead and go," my brother spunked. "When you get it out of your system, you'll be back."

Bob's old company commander, Captain Townsend, encouraged, "If I was a young man, I'd do just that!"

We did.

We both had adventuresome spirits, and anything spelling new places and new experiences appealed to us. As youngsters, Bob and his brother wanted to be commercial fishermen or farmers in the "big country" called Alaska. When they found out they'd have to join the fisherman's union, they decided it wasn't for them. They were far too independent for that.

We were tired of keeping up with the Jones', ladder-climbing, and the rat race of the Lower-48. We read everything we could get our hands on about Alaska, the Land of Opportunity. Because we weren't hung up on conveniences or being away from our families, we felt we could make a living on the frontier.

At Mare Island, California, in September, 1949, the U.S. Marines discharged Bob. We proved to housing inspectors that our apartment was still habitable, then closed the door. I gave up reduced prices on gas, movies, housing, and groceries when I relinquished my commissary card. This was our final link with military life. As I handed the card to the bus driver on my last trip off the base, I had mixed feelings; a tearing away as well as a new beginning. Burning bridges was very uncomfortable, so I concentrated on the bright future.

With our two -year-old, Roger, and his toys and furniture in the car, we steered toward our hometown of Yakima, Washington, pulling a small, two-wheeled trailer loaded with our meager possessions. We waited there from September until April, the target time to begin our trek to Alaska.

In Yakima Valley, we worked picking apples, until Bob started firing boilers on the night shift for the Washington Highway Department. I kept busy canning chicken, peaches, and apple sauce kept extensive notes of tasks to make the upcoming trip pleasant and memorable.

In February, while visiting relatives in Yakima, we noticed a 14-foot, home-made travel trailer under the apple trees in their back yard. Over the years, brush had nearly engulfed it, and dust had accumulated everywhere. We walked around it, pulled the grass away, brushed away the peeling paint, and rubbed dust from the windows. "It's just what we need," Bob said as he kicked a tire. "If it'll do, we won't have to worry about where we'll sleep and eat."

I brushed the dust from my hands, opened the door, and inspected the interior. It had possibilities, and the excitement of a home on wheels made me smile. The price was right—we bought it for $100 cash. We talked far into the night about cost and ways of fixing up our Little Igloo on Wheels.

The next day, we pulled the trailer into an empty lot next to our apartment building and, for the next few months, spent weekends painting and remodeling. I sewed new curtains, slipcovers, and pillow cases. Bob installed bright, new linoleum on the countertop and floor. I stocked closets, built-ins, and cupboards with toys, dishes, clothes, bedding, and groceries. By April, the trailer's interior was snug, warm, and dry, with its new coat of pale, yellow paint.

We traded our small car for a new 3/4-ton Studebaker pickup. Lon, an old friend of the family, was retired and bored stiff. He came over every day for a week and eagerly helped Bob build racks in the pickup bed. Bob was glad for the help. We loaded tools, boxes, trunks, canned goods, spare tires, extra clothing, small appliances, baby furniture, and even an old refrigerator we thought we couldn't get along without in Alaska.

On April Fools Day 1950, a clear and windy spring day, amid sentimental good-byes and good luck wishes from relatives and friends, we left Yakima.

Harold, Bob's brother-in-law, had gathered a small gunny sack full of nuts and bolts and, while we said our good-byes, shoved it into Bob's hands.

"Here, take this. May come in handy before you get to Alaska."

Bob took the sack to be polite, not thinking we'd need them. We piled in and, with $400, Roger, and me, four-months pregnant, Bob turned the truck to the north.

Alaska, here we come!

We spent our first night in the trailer in a vacant lot at Ritzville, Washington, readjusting our load and reinforcing the trailer tongue. Bob murmured, while he dug into the sack for nuts and bolts, "I really didn't think I'd need these so soon."

The following day, at King's Gate, British Columbia, we checked through Canadian Customs, listed everything we owned, and bought a $7 bond to insure passage through Canada. While making the list, we couldn't remember the brand name of our refrigerator, packed near the front of the truck, but knew it started with a C.

The Customs Official said, "Let's go see it."

Bob began to loosen the tarp.

After watching the effort to get the tarp untied from the top and sides of the pickup the Official said, "Lets call it a Crosley," and he marked it off his list.

Two arrogant young men ahead of us had mouthed off to the officials and were being taught a lesson in manners. They had to take everything out of their truck and spread it on the ground; unloading as we got there and still reloading as we left.

That night, we parked on an extra-wide pull-out along the road south of Cranbrook, British Columbia.

The next morning, Bob went across the road to replenish our meager water supply and knocked on the door of a wretched looking little farmhouse. An obese, unkempt woman finally appeared, resenting our intrusion into her poverty-stricken world.

"May I have a bucket of water?" Bob politely asked.

The woman rearranged her dingy hair, grumbled, and led Bob to the well, where he bailed the water using a rope and an old rusty pail.

"Do I owe you anything?" he asked.

"Fifty cents, mister. All you stupid people going to Alaska, who don't have enough sense to haul water, ought to have to pay for it. How come you want to leave America and go to that God-forsaken place?"

Without replying, he left her standing by her well.

Bob sputtered on and on about injustice from such a miserable person, "I'll never pay 50 cents again for a pail of water."

When we arrived at Fernie, British Colombia, we bought a milk can at a hardware store.

The store overflowed with typical frontier items: lamps, tools, nails, roofing, washtubs, clothesline, hand pumps, and fruit jars. As I excitedly looked up and down the aisles, I said, "I hope when we get to Alaska there's a store just like this. But I suppose we'll be buying lots of things we need from catalogs."

The owner of the hardware store tried to talk us into staying in Fernie. "What are you folks going to do in Alaska?"

Bob told him his parents homesteaded in Alberta but that we were going to homestead in Kenai, Alaska.

"You can't be Yankee if your parents homesteaded in Alberta. I knew you were a boy from the prairie," the owner remarked.

After talking about the Canadian prairie, we were afraid our resolve to go on to Alaska had weakened from our love of Fernie, a small friendly town among beautiful rolling hills.

During the next few days, our life settled into a pleasant traveling pattern with candy, ice cream cones, and coffee stops giving us a pleasant respite. Naps every afternoon also lessened the monotony of driving the rough road. While traveling, Roger insisted Bob stop, or at least slow down, to wave at every passing train and airplane. He amused himself, and us, with an old alarm clock and tire pump. He'd take the pump in one hand and, holding the hose with the other, direct the flow of air onto our faces and laugh hilariously as we responded. He learned to wind the alarm clock and, when it went off, hold it to our ears. He also had a cigar box full of odds and ends; treasures for any small boy: paper, pencil, airplanes, tiny toy cars, a small hammer,

Cracker Jack toys, nuts and bolts, and a partial deck of cards, along with a miniature magnet.

In five days, we reached Edmonton. We pulled into a small trailer court and spent the next two days replenishing our supply of groceries, doing the laundry, enjoying hot showers, inspecting our pickup and trailer, and taking in the sights of the town. We visited Eaton's of Canada department store. I bought two Hudson Bay blankets and a bright red snowsuit for Roger. Our trailer court was across the street from a service station. While I stayed in the trailer, Bob worked his way across a muddy road to talk to the owner of the station.

He asked Bob, "Yank, how do you feel about plowing up that line between the United States and Canada and making us one country?"

Bob told him that, as a guest in Canada, he didn't want to say one way or the other.

"I don't care what people think," the man continued. "We should be one country. We talk and think alike and have many of the same political views and interests."

"What would you call the country?" Bob questioned.

"Oh, we're smart enough to think of a name to suit both sides," he quickly responded.

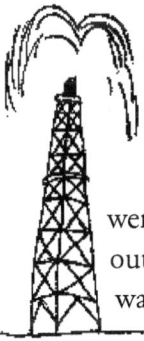

Later, while traveling north, Bob talked to many Canadians who wanted our two countries to become one.

Edmonton was experiencing a booming oil economy. Supply trucks were rushing everywhere. Stores were crowded and restaurants were booming with business. Piles of oil machinery were stacked in muddy lots. Subdivisions were springing up throughout the town like weeds in a garden. We drove around and mud was everywhere. The yards didn't have summer landscaping yet, and roads were almost impassable with muck. All equipment, including school buses and private cars, were coated with mud. Coming from Yakima, a city of sidewalks, paved streets, and manicured lawns, we hoped all the mud ended here and didn't continue on the Alaska Highway. With some misgivings, but with strong determination, we forged ahead. The pavement ended eight miles north of Edmonton and muddy roads began again.

In the Province of Alberta, the road snaked in treacherous curves through mountainous canyons and down into pristine valleys. Mud and water collected on the roads, making travel hazardous during the day. Drivers of cars and trucks formed caravans on hilltops during the afternoon and early evening hours, waiting through the night for freezing spring weather to cool and harden the muddy spots in the road. The caravans would generally start traveling again around 4 AM.

A homesteader with a team of horses waited at one troublesome spot to pull cars and trucks through the sticky mud. He was charging $10 for his towing services. One by one, each vehicle attempted to plough through the mud and ooze. Some made it, some didn't. One driver of our awaiting caravan swore the homesteader was spending all night letting water back into the mud hole so he could swindle motorists by charging them for pulling their vehicles through the mire.

When our turn came, Bob threw the truck into gear and said, "Hang on. Here we go."

If I hadn't been pregnant, and with a two -year-old in tow, I'd have insisted on walking down that hill and up the other side, meeting Bob at the top. What a ride! We slid, bumped, slipped, and splashed through the mud hole to dryer ground.

"Look at that crook! He's shaking his fist at us!" Bob chuckled as he looked in the rear view mirror. "He didn't get our $10!"

A few hours later, we arrived in Dawson Creek, mile zero of the Alaska Highway. We didn't linger in Dawson, just cleaned the sticky, black mud from the trailer and truck, and purchased a tank of gas, along with a few groceries.

We stopped in Fort St. John, 50 miles further on, to have a registered seal put on Bob's rifle because we were driving through a National Park. While there, we had the trailer hitch welded. It kept working loose and the valuable sack of nuts and bolts given to us by Harold was almost empty.

In a wild, remote section of the Yukon Territory, the trailer swung wildly behind us. The left wheel went careening into a small pond. The axle gouged the roadbed and drew us to a complete stop. A bearing on the trailer wheel was ground to small pieces. The spindle attached to the wheel was chewed and burred and damage was severe. We had to replace the entire axle. We were miles from any town or auto service. After mulling over the situation, we decided to leave the trailer beside the road. In the dust on the back trailer window we wrote, "We'll be back soon," hoping to discourage theft or vandalism.

We planned to go on to Alaska, or the nearest help, secure the needed axle parts, and return to the trailer. We stashed food, a rifle, and some bedding, in the cab of the pickup, along with two tired people and one restless, energetic child. I looked back feeling like I was leaving a child or a pet by the side of a lonely stretch of uncharted road and I'd never see it again.

A mile or so down the road, we came upon a detachment of Canadian Army soldiers repairing a bridge across the Donjek River. Canadian Army Engineers were in charge of the labor for building the Alaska Highway. Soldiers were idly waiting arrival of parts for repairing the bridge.

"We'd better stop and tell those guys we're leaving our axle-broken trailer beside the road," I suggested.

A half-dozen soldiers, who were lazying in the sunshine, listened placidly to our tale of woe.

The First Sergeant said, "Now don't be so hasty. Let's look the situation over. Maybe we can do something."

Then he, the company clerk, and Bob drove back to inspect the damaged axle. They spent a couple of days driving to other camps looking for another axle. We spent the two nights in the trailer, alongside the road, one side hoisted onto blocks. It was almost impossible for me to sleep because trucks thundered by during the night. I heard them coming long before they arrived. They nearly sucked us into their wake of diesel fumes and flying stones. It seemed like every few minutes I'd wake Bob to tell him, "How can you sleep so sound? Here comes another one!"

When the men finally found an axle, in an army dump, the First Sergeant and the company clerk volunteered a handful of privates and corporals to replace the broken axle.

Roger and I stayed at the mess hall during the day, while the men worked on the axle. Roger was the center of attention. The men missed their families and Roger was a reminder of home. Of course, he showed off too. Unaccustomed to having a woman and a child in camp, they had a difficult time cleaning up their colorful language, often apologizing for a slip of the tongue.

Bob tried to pay them for helping us. They refused all offers.

"Your breakdown kept us busy," they said. We were amazed to find free help here in this wilderness.

We reluctantly left the army camp. In spite of our trouble, we enjoyed the meals and the camaraderie. Now, whenever we travel the Alaska Highway, we watch for the old Army campsite and talk fondly of kind soldiers helping us fix a broken axle. Brush, weeds, and a few bare gravel spots are all that remain of the once thriving military detachment placed there to repair an old rickety, wooden bridge; and our little trailer. A modern steel structure now spans the Donjek River.

All along the Alaska Highway, Canadians told us about construction of the Highway. They started the road in 1942, spurred on by the threat of an invasion from Japan. They told us of bulldozers sinking out of sight into the mud and sections of road disappearing into the muskeg. Some sections of the road had to be rerouted on the upper slopes of the valleys to avoid the treacherous muskeg. Canadian and United States Army personnel, plus many civilians hired by private contractors, built the highway.

We marveled at the massive mobilization of men and equipment it took to construct over 1,500 miles of road through this remote wilderness of lakes, swamps, rivers, forests, and mountains. Several contractors worked on different sections of road at the same time, trying to complete the highway before winter set in. They built the road in eight months. It was barely passable by winter, so work continued, often in temperatures of -50°.

As warmer weather arrived, they had to resurface and gravel sections of the road, install permanent bridges, improve steep grades and sharp curves and add culverts and guard rails. We remember many miles of road winding and zigzagging on fairly flat ground. We later learned the zigzagging gave the enemy less chance of striking a convoy traveling on the road.

By 1950, the road was eight years old. We thought it was rough going for us, but the lodge owners along the way said we should have seen it a few years before, when it was a real nightmare. Lodges and other tourist facilities were built mostly from army camp buildings, which could be bought for next to nothing.

Some nights, we parked our rig at a lodge. Even though we weren't staying in the lodge, it gave us an opportunity to fill the gas tank, check tires, buy bread and fresh milk (if available), and hear the daily road report. I filled my daily exercise requirements at these lodges too. Roger rode his tricycle through every mud hole he could find, and I dashed breathlessly after him.

Starting at Dawson Creek, road builders placed white posts every mile along the ditch banks. Starting with the number zero, they numbered the mileposts consecutively, until we reached the Alaska border. Maintenance crews used the mileposts as landmarks in this vast wilderness to help identify where they needed to repair the road. Occasionally, one was missing. Sometimes the mileposts were stolen as souvenirs, perhaps as a bleak reminder of trouble encountered.

Occasionally, we saw small white crosses at the side of the road. Some times a cross stood alone, sometimes crosses huddled in groups, grimly reminding us of tragic accidents and death of loved ones.

As we traveled north, the land returned to the grip of winter. Cabins looked deserted, even though there was smoke unfurling from chimneys. Most lodges were shut down for the winter. Snow was everywhere. Each day the sun melted the ice and snow, and little rivers of water began to run everywhere. At times, we saw people with a hoe or shovel, ditching the water away from buildings.

One day, as we rounded a curve and were about to drive up a steep hill, we noticed a truck at the top being unhooked from a huge tractor. The morning sun's direct rays had melted just enough ice on the hill to cause extremely slippery conditions. The tractor had pulled the truck up the slope.

We were slowly inching our way up the hill, when our trailer jockeyed perilously close to the edge of the cliff. Panicked, Bob pumped and pumped the brakes, then said through clenched teeth, "The brakes won't hold on this ice! We're going backwards! The cliff—." (He used unprintable expletives)

I couldn't imagine what would happen if we went over. I held Roger close to me and bit my lip. My mind went blank just as the truck and trailer jack-knifed and saved itself on a patch of gravel. We shakily got out of the truck, I clutching Roger, while Bob surveyed our dilemma.

The homesteader with the tractor hollered, "Stay put. I'll pull you to the top when I'm finished here." He went back to helping with the truck.

Bob located his truck chains behind the cab seat and began laying them out on the icy road. As I watched, he'd slip to one knee or try to stand steady, again and again. The homesteader worked his way to our rig to help Bob, took over, and, without gloves, put the chains on the tires easily and quickly. It was +20°.

"How can you work without gloves?" I asked. "Don't your hands freeze? It's so blasted cold!"

"It's not that cold," he pleasantly replied. "Are you going to Alaska to live?"

"Yes, we are."

"Well, you just wait and see. After you've lived in Alaska for a while, you'll get used to the cold and you'll think plus-20° is warm."

I hoped what he said was true. (It was.)

We were nervous wrecks by the time we slowly and cautiously drove the next 60 icy miles to a lodge with complete garage facilities. We had the brakes repaired and, early the following morning, were on our way again, beginning day 13 of travel.

Our trailer bounced and bobbed along behind us. The scenery changed from farmlands to wooded areas of lodgepole pine and spruce. Ponds in the meadows were still icebound. Small log cabins were scattered here and there. Smoke drifting from the chimneys made us contemplate the hard and lonely existence of the occupants. Flying stones from the wheels of passing trucks did their share of damage to our rig—a cracked windshield and broken headlights. Oncoming traffic automatically caused us to flinch, awaiting a hail of little stones.

Good fortune, however, was with us for the remainder of the trip, and lunch stops along the road were in valleys bathed in warm, spring sun. The sun set later every evening and rose earlier every morning. Spring was following us north.

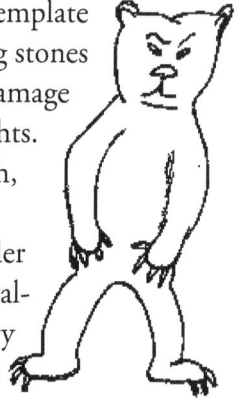

This was rugged country; a land where, while looking at snowdrifts in the woods, you could be stuck in the mud on the road and have dust blown in your face.

The countryside changed again and became flat and boggy with low, scrubby, stunted trees and dried grasses. Amid this scenery we traveled mile after weary mile.

The only break in our routine was an occasional flat tire or a fox or rabbit crossing the road. Once, while Bob changed a tire, we watched a mother bear with cubs play alongside the road.

'Fresh Bread' scrawled on a small sign pointed to a rustic cabin surrounded by birch and spruce. Smoke gently wafted from the chimney. It tugged at our curiosity.

"Bob, can we stop a minute? We need bread, and it's a good chance for a rest," I stated, anticipating an adventure.

As we pulled into the yard, we saw bear and moose hides nailed to the outside of the cabin. A sign on the door invited, "Please Come In."

We entered one large room, the back half separated from the front by a counter displaying snacks, candy bars, and huge loaves of bread. The walls on the inside of the cabin were lined with wolf pelts.

A woman with twinkling, brown eyes and a bubbly personality, dressed in Levis and a wool shirt with sleeves rolled up, poked more wood into her old-fashioned, wood-burning cook stove. She turned and greeted us as she brushed the top of the fresh, warm loaves of bread with melted butter. The heat from the stove and the aroma of the freshly-baked bread radiated throughout the cabin.

"Where you from?" the woman asked as she wiped her hands on a muslin apron.

"We're from Washington and headed to Alaska. We think we're going to be homesteaders."

"Homesteading is what I do best," she laughed. "I cut my own wood, haul my own water, and bake bread for visitors. I even shoot and dress out bear, moose, and wolves when they're brave enough to get into my sights. Why, I bait bears by putting my hot apple pies on the window ledge to cool. The bears can't resist. I don't even have to leave my bread baking, I just plug them through the window from right here in my own little kitchen."

She delighted us with tales of life in the wilderness. She told about a Canadian soldier working on the Donjek River Bridge who had asked her to marry him. He met her while on maneuvers in Alaska. He was involved in some kind of money-making scheme, probably gambling in Alaska. Canadians couldn't take more than $500 out of the country unless they were married to an American. Needless to say, she turned down his proposal.

After a bottle of soda pop, we were on our way again, thoroughly refreshed by this pleasant interlude. At suppertime, we parked alongside the road, in a gravel pit near Tok Junction, then an Alaska border town. We dined on thick slabs of fresh bread smothered with cold butter and my homemade raspberry jam. This was an added treat to a can of chicken noodle soup. We spent the night there.

The next morning, United States Customs Officials asked us a few questions, took a quick look at legal documents, and sent us on our way. How exciting it was to know we were so close to dreams which had sustained us since leaving Washington.

Trappers, just in from the bush, met at the lodges to sell their fox, beaver, and muskrat pelts, and exchange stories. They were delighted with Roger's charm and friendliness. At Gakona Lodge, a trapper gave him a silver dollar. The trapper was a rough-talking character with a gentle way about him. Just coming from a winter in the bush, he had long hair and a tobacco-stained beard. His clothes were dirty, and he never stopped telling his tales of the great North.

Forty years later, we gave the silver dollar to Roger, a souvenir of his first adventure on the Alaska Highway.

Three more days of bleak, snowless landscapes gave way to log barns and farmhouses nestled against towering mountains touched with snow. The air was bursting with the smells of spring, mosquitoes were beginning to be a nuisance, and mud was everywhere.

The April sun was coaxing leaves onto the trees. The wild Matanuska River, fed by towering glaciers, Cathedral Mountain, white with alabaster streaks, the forested hills and silt-filled streams were scenes right out of a Robert Service poem. We were home.

Our original destination was the Kenai Peninsula. As we got closer to Anchorage, folks told us there was no road to the peninsula, so we changed our plans and decided the first community we came to which could provide us employment would be the place to settle down.

On April 23rd, we arrived in Palmer, Alaska. We journeyed 23 days and 3,000 miles of muddy, twisting, rocky roads, encountering steep cliffs, and low valleys. We met trappers, homesteaders, and lodge owners, and Martha—who could shoot a bear from her kitchen window.

First Summer

We paid $5 rent for a week at a trailer court on the edge of Palmer, unhitched the trailer, had sandwich for lunch, then took a leisurely tour of the valley, from Knik River to Wasilla.

Palmer is located 45 miles north of Anchorage. During the 1930s, 180 farmers from the Midwest colonized here under the Alaska Rural Rehabilitation Corporation, a federal program, to help families suffering from the depression. This was a valley with a 120-day growing season, rich fertile soil, and nearly 24 hours of daylight during the summer. I couldn't believe my eyes. I was thrilled with the resemblance of this neat farm area to Washington. It looked almost like home. It suggested freedoms I had dreamed of, and it hinted of adventure that I looked forward to. It didn't take long for me to feel comfortable. Bob was not the least bit unhappy with the beautiful Matanuska Valley, and the more we looked around, the more we were convinced this place would be a good home.

We had $60 to our name when we arrived in Palmer. Our gaunt finances dictated Bob seek employment. Early the next morning, he drove into Anchorage. He inquired at the Alaska Road Commission for employment, but to no avail.

He located the Employment Office and sauntered up to the receptionist and said, "Is this the unemployment office?"

"No, this is the employment office," she snapped.

He received the usual reply—Don't call us, we'll call you—and then went down the street to a jewelry store.

"My watch needs cleaning," he said to the jeweler. "Can you do it for me?"

The jeweler snarled, "I'll decide if your watch is dirty. Don't tell me how to run my business."

Bob yanked the watch from the jeweler's hand, jammed it into his pocket, and slammed the door on his way out. He then walked to a real estate office to see if our trailer could be sold on consignment. The lady questioned how much he wanted for it.

Bob answered, "$300."

"If that's all you want for it," the lady growled, "it's probably no good for nothing."

Bob stormed out of her office, mad again. This inhospitable treatment wasn't part of our dream picture of this new land and people. To top it off, on the way home, he had a flat tire.

When he entered our trailer, he leaned against the counter where I was stirring soup, and said to me, with a dejected look, "I wish I'd stayed in bed this morning."

That same night, Bob had a nightmare. He dreamed he was still driving the Alaska Highway.

In his dream, as the guard rail of a bridge loomed in front of him, he hollered, "I'm going to hit it!"

I sat straight up in bed and yelled back, "Stop the truck!"

The head of our bed was below a small window in the trailer. In his dream, he imagined the trailer window was the windshield of the pickup. In agitation, Bob jammed his foot to the brake. The abrupt jerk of his leg smashed his head against the window. Shattered glass flew everywhere. Bob got up and didn't say a word, while I spluttered and cleaned the splinters from our bed. Early the next morning, he humbly picked up the pieces of broken glass lying in the yard. Bob was afraid the neighbors would think we'd had a domestic quarrel.

After his fitful sleep, but with a cheerful attitude, he went job hunting again, this time in Palmer. The first job he asked for was at the Matanuska Valley Farmer's Cooperative Association.

"Would one day's work help?" the boss asked.

"It sure would!" Bob grinned from ear to ear.

The next morning, Bob reported for work at the maintenance department. He worked there for the next nine months.

Two weeks after our arrival in Palmer, a spry, plumpish, middle-aged woman stepped up to us in the Co-op grocery store. A bright bandana covered her graying, curly hair. Her clean, cotton dress, knee-high boots, and mackinaw jacket told us she was dressed adequately for her weekly trip to town. Her name was Annie Wilson. As we got to know her, we began to refer to her as the valley matriarch. She was interested in everyone and always had an answer for current problems. Her husband, Ty, was almost deaf, so her voice was naturally loud.

She began to quiz us. "You must be new in town," Annie crackled loudly. We told her we were looking for a house to rent.

"I have a small, two -room cabin," Annie interjected. "I could rent it to you for $25 a month. It has no electricity. You'll have to bail well water. The man who owns it is living in our house, with me and my husband, for the time being. He's bed-ridden with cancer, and it's just a matter of time before he passes on. The cabin will be available then. Besides, I need a family to buy my eggs and fresh milk." Annie gave us detailed instructions on how to get to her place then patted my arm and shuffled off, hollering at other friends.

Eager to find a house to rent, we jumped at her proposal. "We'll come out this evening and look at it," we hollered after her. She waved to us from her other conversations.

We went to our Little Igloo on Wheels in the trailer court, and made plans to move into Annie's cabin, sight unseen. Two weeks later, we drove the trailer into the yard of our new home. We continued to live in the trailer for another week, until we could get the old cabin livable.

The two-room cabin was located 17 miles from Palmer, on the Cottonwood Road, now known as Fairview Loop Road. It was situated on a rise of ground in a small clearing. The cabin had a rickety old porch nailed across the front. No one had lived in the cabin for some time and it was dank, dusty, and smelly. The front room had one window. An old-fashioned, dilapi- dated, wood-burning cookstove had a counter next to it which held a water bucket and wash basin. A front-loading wood box was built into the counter. An old, wooden table with peeling paint was nestled in one corner, and an old chair was tipped over in another. The walls had been papered at one time, but they were faded, peeling, and hadn't been cleaned for years.

The back room was dimly lit by a large, dirty window. An

old, kerosene-burning, incubator sat in the middle of the floor. I sighed, just thinking of the work it would take to get this tiny cabin clean enough for Bob, Roger, and me. The out buildings were weather-beaten, but serviceable. There was a well with a rusty pail and worn rope, immediately reminding me of the stingy woman who charged us 50 cents for a pail of water. I walked into the yard and immediately recognized an area for a garden. In my mind, I began clearing, tilling, and planting.

Bob replaced the rusted lengths of stovepipe with new ones purchased at the general store in Wasilla. I helped him move the incubator into one of the out-buildings. I washed the two large windows looking out on the mountains to the south.

We hung clothing from a makeshift pole attached to a wall of the bedroom. We stored other clothing in boxes under Roger's crib, and hung our outdoor jackets on nails near the door, with our boots on a rug under them. I cleaned walls and prettied up inside the cabin. After applying soapy water and scrubbing the dirty floor with a mop, a pretty pattern emerged. I washed it again and shined it with wax. I hung pictures and colorful curtains, placed rag rugs, and stored groceries in the open cupboards, which Bob had repaired.

Bob filled the wood box, cleaned the debris from the yard, and put up a clothesline between two trees. He took his cross-cut saw, went into the woods, and cut seven stumps, each about 18 inches high. We used six as legs for a mattress and springs Annie loaned us. We used the other as a chair for Roger. Years later, he lamented about throwing away his stump chair.

Annie scrounged another chair from one of her out-buildings. It was dusty and needed repair, but, after fixing it, it was nice to have two chairs. After living in the tiny trailer for nearly tw0 months, we thought the cabin was a palace.

While we were busy upgrading the cabin, Annie came over to make sure we knew about her shrew bucket in a hole in the ground near the well. Annie's shrew trap was a five-gallon metal bucket buried with the top level with the surrounding ground.

Shrews are mouse-like animals, with elongated tails and more pointed noses than mice. They're nervous, panicky animals, with a ferocious appetite. They're digestive systems require food in them all times or they'll starve.

A shrew will run aimlessly until it falls into the bucket, unable to get out. Sooner or later another shrew falls into the trap. Being a carnivorous creature, one will eat the other. This process goes on forever. You know how many shrews are trapped by counting tails still left in the bucket.

Instead of payment of the first month's rent, Bob wired the cabin for electricity. Bob knew nothing about electricity, but he took this project in stride, consulting knowledgeable friends for advice.

The rickety, old stove was a constant hazard and worry. It was rusty and unreliable, so we took $200 and went to Anchorage, not really expecting to find the combination electric and wood-burning stove we needed. At Northern Commercial Company, we found a kitchen range with four electric burners, and an area almost as large as the burners, for wood. It was the only stove left in their inventory and they were glad to part with it. I was delighted! I didn't have to baby-sit an old, unreliable stove after banking the hot coals at night. I no longer had to fear burning the cabin down.

While Bob was working at the Co-op, we met Leo Nunley, a Navy veteran, and Tom Nail, an ex-Marine paratrooper, who encouraged us to join the VFW. They recruited other veteran homesteaders in our area to join. It became an excellent way to get acquainted with people through socializing, community activities, and supporting the veterans projects. Meetings were held in the Wasilla School, now the city office building.

Our neighbors, Ralph Bradley and Herb Holstein, had been good friends for many years and they were like two peas in a pod. They did everything together. They even thought the same way and were both fun-loving, cheerful, and extra friendly to us. They were interested in us becoming successful farmers. They took us in like long lost kittens. They were delighted to have new friends and a new audience for their old stories.

Jewel, Herb's wife, immediately became my friend. Her pleasant, genuine laugh embraced my heart and made me feel cheery. The first thing she'd do each morning was apply her eye makeup. She was then ready to face a new day. She walked with a limp, due to a hip injury. She loved our kids and often brought them cookies. She also gave us our first dog, Pepper.

Pat, Ralph's wife, was neat and dainty, with a kind, cheerful face. She was quiet in nature, but always helpful with information. She gave the kids their first kitten, Bobo. Her garden and greenhouse were her quiet hobbies. Pat and Jewel were a never-ending source of information, advice, and friendship.

At the end of May, it was time to start planting a garden. I sought advice from them about which vegetables would grow and how much fertilizer to apply.

As a novice at gardening, I planted peas, beans, lettuce, cabbage, onions, carrots, potatoes, radishes, Swiss chard, and green beans. The long hours of summer sunlight and plenty of rain caused the vegetables— including weeds—to grow into giants. Bob weeded from the time supper was over until I hollered at him. "Bob, it's 11 o'clock. Quit and come to bed. You've got to go to work in the morning."

He'd brush the dirt from his hands, murmuring, "I didn't know it was so late."

One evening, we took Roger and went visiting Herb and Jewel. While we were there, Herb's cow got into Annie's commercial lettuce field.

"Let's get that cow out of there. Annie will have a fit!" shouted Herb. The men whistled as they ran across the road into the field. The women began shouting, "Here boss, here boss." With all the hubbub, the cow got nervous and confused and thrashed through the lettuce helter skelter, damaging everything in her path.

In his anger, Herb bellered to his wife, "Get the damn gun. I'll shoot the cow!" The cow was eventually corralled.

The next morning, two young calves strayed into our yard. Roger, seeing them from the kitchen window, hollered, "Get the damn gun, Daddy, and shoot the cows."

During July and August, raspberries were abundant along ditches and roadsides. I picked all I wanted around our cabin and along the road to Annie's place. I put Roger to bed around 8 PM, leaving Bob in charge. In the remaining daylight hours, I picked berries.

As I accumulated berries, I imagined the jars lining my shelves, waiting for winter treats. I made enough jelly and jam to last a year.

At harvesttime, Bob, Roger, and I, walked the half-mile to Annie's house to pay the rent. Annie and Ty, along with a small crew, were digging potatoes. The crew was yelling and throwing potatoes at Ty, who was driving the tractor. It took a minute for us to figure out the crew's abuse. Ty was almost deaf, and they needed to signal him when to stop the tractor so they could clean the digger of vines and debris. Throwing potatoes got his attention.

Salmon were abundant in Fish Creek, located about 20 miles from our house. Salmon were so thick during spawning season, you could almost walk across the creek on their backs. Bob, Pat, Ralph, and I traveled to Fish Creek and got our share of the delicious salmon.

Families from neighboring towns camped in cars, tents, and campers, for days at a time on the creek bank. Small fires burned along the creek all night, acrid smoke floating into the air. The men snagged fish and the women canned them, using the water from the creek. We took our fish home and canned them the next day. I had my own utensils and I knew my water supply was good.

People from all over came to Fish Creek. They came for recreation rather than to get a winter's supply of salmon. They attempted to give away their snagged salmon. They caught the salmon and threw them on the bank. Soon, the hot sun and the flies made them unfit for human consumption. I'm glad laws have been put into place since then to save the spawning salmon.

I bought a pressure cooker and two dozen jars in Wasilla. I'd never used a pressure cooker before and followed the instructions carefully. Once, when the pressure gauge went higher than the recommended 10 pounds, I shoved the cooker to the back of the stove and pulled Roger to me under the kitchen table, hoping it was the safest place. I'd heard of one homesteader's wife who's cooker exploded, sending chicken everywhere. She cleaned up chicken parts from walls and ceiling for several days, threw away her cooker, and vowed never to use it again.

First Winter

After fishing season came and went, it was time to get serious about canning and preserving our garden harvest Gardening had been work all summer, with bugs, weeds, and wet weather. I was close to delivering our second child. I panted and puffed while hoeing and watering, but I loved it. I felt a glow of security and accomplishment. The reward was eating to our heart's content, such things as peas, lettuce, carrots, and broccoli, along with chard and potatoes.

Most of the hard garden work was over by August 1st. I canned peas, green beans, Swiss chard, and pickled carrots into dozens of fruit jars. The cabin had a root cellar below a trap door in the center of the kitchen floor, where we stored enough carrots, turnips, potatoes, rutabagas, and canned goods to keep us through the winter.

Before our second baby was born, we purchased some undershirts, diapers, and one "uptown," or best, blanket. Friends donated the remainder of the clothes. It was common practice to pass around used baby clothes to whoever could use them.

On August 26th, Barbara Ann, seven pounds, 12 ounces, was born. She was a healthy baby, with red hair and bright eyes. Dr. Cates encouraged Bob to stay in the delivery room and watch. He believed it didn't hurt any man to see a baby born. After her birth, Dr. Cates laid her on her stomach on a table while Bob watched. She arched her back and seemed to look around. I don't suppose she could see, but she was a strong little baby. At this time, Barbara and Bob formed a special bond that has lasted through the years.

Here we were, at the beginning of our first winter in Alaska, and we never had it so good. We were free from military pressures and snugly comfortable in our little log cabin. Our second child was born healthy and strong. We were contentedly enjoying frontier living.

We fell in love with the frozen beauty of Alaska during our first winter. The outdoor winter wonderland with heavy snow piled high was a photographer's paradise. Snow-blanketed Chugach Mountains stood out in breath-taking sunset hues of pink and gold. The sky, glacier-ice blue, with scudding clouds, added to the magic of this unique country.

When it snowed in significant amounts, Bob piled the loose snow to a depth of two feet around the foundation of the cabin. This served as insulation and prevented possible drafts. Bob bought the smallest oil stove he could find and set it up in a corner of the kitchen. With a new baby who demanded night feedings, it was a real pleasure to have the cabin warm, even on the coldest of winter nights. On clear, moonlit nights, I never bothered turning on a light in the cabin as I heated her bottle and fed her. Often, I moved my chair to our large, front room window to watch moose browsing in our yard. I felt tender feelings for these giants of the woods. They symbolized a hardy nature and an acceptance of the harsh environment. I felt at peace living in their territory. The moose accepted its life as I did mine.

I soon became an expert at cooking on a wood-burning stove, and I also learned how to bank a fire for the night. Banking a fire is a talent, if it can be mastered. A deep bed of hot ashes is first leveled off in the firebox. A large chunk of wood is then laid on top of the ashes, with a few smaller pieces of wood laid around the larger one. Then, all drafts are closed. The lack of air keeps these ashes hot and, hopefully, doesn't set the wood on fire. The best way to learn the art of banking a fire is through trial and error. The next morning, all the drafts are opened. With the rush of air to the ashes and dry wood, the flames erupt into a full-blown fire.

Bob was the first person up in the morning when the alarm sounded. Opening the stovepipe damper to adjust the air intake, and adding kin-

dling and a few heavier sticks of wood, he'd soon have a hot fire. I'd struggle into my robe and slippers, hoping the rooms would be half as warm as my bed. We'd soon have water boiling. The kids would begin clamoring to be up for the day. While I heated a bottle of milk for the baby, Roger would attempt to get dressed. Breakfast was usually pancakes or hot cereal. I made Bob's lunch and pushed him out the door. I began my daily tasks and worked most of the morning.

When the kids went down for their naps, I'd do things in which I didn't want their help. I wrote many letters to family and friends, did hand sewing, or tried a favorite recipe. Sometimes, I'd take a nap myself. Occasionally, I'd have a new book from the library and, with a couple of cookies, I'd settle down to read and not budge until the kids woke up.

The local country store in Wasilla sold washing machines, and I admired one for months before we bought one on time payments. Bob drew a regular paycheck, so it wasn't much of a sacrifice to pay for one. My shiny, new wringer washing machine did a fantastic job of washing clothes. Doing laundry while living in the cabin wasn't hard work. I did some laundry by hand, but it was very little. I was grateful to kind neighbors who let me use their washing machines until I became the proud owner of a machine my own.

I'd winch enough water from the well to fill a wash-boiler sitting on the hot stove. The hot water was for the washer and while it was heating, I'd put cold water into another tub for rinsing.

If the water wasn't too dirty after five loads of clothes, I took a bucketful of the hot, soapy water and scrubbed the kitchen floor with a mop. I scrubbed the floor and bench of the outhouse with a broom and remaining water, but kept the moose hide-lined seat dry. We really appreciated the fur-lined seat on cold, winter mornings.

One day, when Barbara was about three months old, I told Roger I was going outside to hang diapers on the line. "I want you to watch Barbara. I don't want her to fall on the floor," I called from the door.

She was lying on a cot in the kitchen, content as could be, engrossed in the wonder of discovering her hands. Roger was nearby, playing with his toys. When I returned to the cabin and opened the door, the baby was lying on the floor, still just as happy as could be.

"I told you to watch her," I scolded.

"I did," he shouted back at me. "I watched her fall on the floor."

With a new baby, I had to wash diapers at least twice a week. When the weather was nice, I hung them outside to dry. During the winter it seemed we had wall-to-wall diapers. At times, I rushed the season and hung the clothes outside while there was still snow on the ground. The clothes smelled like fresh air and sunshine.

All winter, we watched moose scavenging on the remains of our garden. These huge, silent, fascinating animals were always a joy to watch. They had high shoulders, slender legs, and huge heads with ears to match.

The snow was exceptionally deep that first winter. We were snowed in for days at a time. Consequently, Bob couldn't get to work. The snow plow always seemed to plow our road last.

During these times, I concentrated on my usual domestic chores. Laundry, ironing, and baking bread were easier with the radio playing or neighbors visiting. Bob spent his time with Ralph and Herb, vainly attempting to get each other's pickups started.

"Why are you doing it?" I asked. "You can't go anywhere."

Heavy snowfall blocked the roads. They knew they weren't going anywhere, but it kept them busy. Most of the time, they complained about the weather, split and carried wood for each other's stoves, or retreated often to each other's cabin for coffee and warmth.

Homesteader's Season—an illegal—but accepted moose hunting time, was open all winter. Homesteaders took advantage of the season to fill their freezers. I don't recall hearing of anyone shooting an animal, then wasting the meat.

The Alaska Department of Fish and Game wasn't real strict during this season. "We know what you're doing, just don't brag about it. Don't sell the meat, and don't leave a blood trail. Above all, don't waste the meat."

We knew if they caught anyone, they'd have to, by law, prosecute. They could fine, confiscate weapons, and maybe give jail time.

We needed meat, so Bob was on the look out for a barren moose cow crossing our property.

Ralph was visiting us one wintery afternoon. Snow was falling heavily and, just before dusk, a big moose wandered into our garden to dig the remains of delicious turnips, cabbage, and rutabagas. Bob shot it and the men helplessly watched it fall at the far end of the drive

way, near the road. The men panicked. They decided an old, white tarp and the heavy falling snow would cover the moose, keeping it undetected as they harvested the meat.

When the school bus came lumbering down the road, the men stopped cleaning the moose, quickly threw the tarp over it, piled snow around it, and dove for the nearby brush. When the bus continued on, the men, hidden by the dense falling snow, finished the harvesting.

Ralph went home, to return after dark to help Bob hang the moose in the old barn. Bob got restless and didn't wait, retrieving the moose by himself. Muscling 800 pounds of meat took his whole attention. He wrestled with the hindquarters and finally hung them from the rafters. He was preparing to hang the front quarters when Ralph and Herb drove into the yard.

The men quietly approached the barn, then banged loudly on the door. "Hey, what's going on in there?" Bob turned off the light and scrambled for the door. He thought the law was after him and envisioned spending the winter in jail. He crashed into Ralph and Herb as he bolted through the door. All three laughed and went back to finish the job. They never let Bob forget the incident, and laughed uproariously every time they retold it.

I'll never forget the thrill of having all that moose meat. I learned how to can meat. I scanned my cookbooks and adapted the beef dishes and found they tasted better with moose. We ate moose stew, steak, roast, chili, meatballs, spaghetti, Stroganoff, mincemeat, and ground meat. We never tired of the taste of the robust, red meat.

We were guilt-ridden all winter after Bob's illegal escapade, and listened for ADFG airplanes or the heavy hand of the law. We burned the moose bones so no evidence could be found. We felt sure anyone driving past our cabin could smell the smoke coming from the chimney.

One blustery, winter day, as I was canning moose meat, a car drove into our yard. The United States Commissioner, May Carter, and Rose Johnson, from Wasilla, came to get my signature on membership forms for the local VFW post. I invited them into the cabin. They got my signature, visited for a few minutes, then went back to Wasilla.

I didn't mention that I was in the middle of canning moose meat. I was a little apprehensive, because I didn't know whether the Commissioner might arrest me. I had no reason to fear. She must have known we were in need of meat and may have done the same in her time of need.

The short, winter days passed quickly. Clear, moonlit-nights with moose browsing in our garden and their crunch, as they walked on the hard-crusted snow, were Alaska pleasures.

Bob nailed a wooden apple box onto Roger's sled and almost every afternoon, weather permitting, I took both kids for a ride in the fresh, clean air and enjoyed the snow and beautiful winter sunshine.

Our first Alaska Christmas was very simple. I ordered toys, candy, and clothes from Sears and Roebuck. During the holidays, we attended school and church programs, where the kids received sacks of goodies. We had a tiny tree decorated with ornaments we'd brought to Alaska. Of course, I baked the usual Christmas pies, fudge, cookies, and fruitcake. It was a reflective time too. I was thankful Bob had a job, the two kids were healthy, and we were living in a warm and comfortable Alaska cabin.

In January 1951, Bob heard the Bureau of Reclamation was hiring laborers to slash a right-of-way for a new transmission line from the old hydro-electric facility near the village of Eklutna to the city of Palmer. He left the Co-op and hired on with the Bureau. He wasn't a surveyor, so he helped with the slashing. The crew chopped and sawed timber from a strip so the surveyor could get a straight line with a transit. He also pulled chain, when necessary. The chain is a measuring line 100 feet long. The snow was up to their waists and the temperature was -20 at times. Stewart, a temporary hire, was the surveyor, and often had one of the crew operate the transit while he slashed brush and timber as a way to get warm again. Although Stewart was born in Alaska, he had to go to the Lower-48 to be permanently hired, then the company transferred him back to work in the Territory. Though he was born in Alaska, he couldn't get a permanent job with the Bureau because Alaska, still a Territory, was treated like a foreign country by the government.

Each day, during the winter, the men came down from the mountains at 3 PM. The days were so short they couldn't climb around in the dark. It was the same in the morning going up, except it would take longer, so they didn't get many actual working hours.

An older man with only one lung was working on one of the crews. As he struggled to climb the mountain to the job site, the men could tell he wouldn't last too long. He lasted a day-and-a-half. He was heavy, and couldn't walk very well because of his bulk. The men had to pack him down the mountain, which was almost straight up and down. He was short of breath and nearly unconscious. He looked like dead, but he survived and was sent back to Denver at government expense.

After the crew worked their way through the deep snow along the mountains to the job site, they ran a line down the mountain, across the Knik River, over the swampy area, and into Palmer. If the crew thought it was cold on the mountain, they were mistaken. In the lowland, it got bitter cold. Some days, it was -30°. Bob kept his feet warm by wearing felt-lined Russian boots inside snow pacs he'd purchased from Eaton's of Canada.

Now, in large cottonwood timber, it took longer to slash the line and was harder work. The snow was still waist deep.

On the crew, Don, a pot-bellied, broad-beamed man, was a newcomer, or cheechako, to Alaska and was unfamiliar with winter conditions in the woods. He didn't have the slightest idea how to handle an axe. When he swung at a tree, he brought the axe up into a figure eight and then to the tree. With this extra motion, he couldn't hit the same spot twice. He'd work himself into a sweat and end up with his whiskers and eyebrows frosty from his puffing. On his third day, about dark, as the men were walking to their cars, they discovered

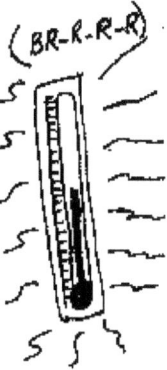

Don wasn't with them. He'd lagged behind. They had to find him or he'd freeze to death. They backtracked nearly a mile, constantly yelling his name. There was no answer, and it was too dark to see him. Bob was on his way back out, when he saw a dark object up against a large tree. He knew it had to be Don. Bob yelled for the men.

Then Bob snapped at him, "You damned fool! We should've left you here to freeze."

The crew had a hard time getting Don to move. Frost covered his face, and he was exhausted. They finally got him back to the vehicles. He never went back into the woods, but worked an office job until he could be sent back to Denver.

For weeks, the weather was bitterly cold. The temperatures ranged from zero at mountain top to -25° at the base. The men's food was frozen solid by midday. Each noon, they built a fire to warm themselves and thaw their sandwiches.

Moose were plentiful in the area. The men had heard of Bob's homestead moose and shouted every time they saw one.

"Hey, Bob, there's a moose. Hurry! Get two slices of bread and make a sandwich."

As cold as it was, and as hard as Bob worked, he was never sick. He'll always remember that job. It took tough men to run a line, and those who couldn't handle it, didn't last. Bob enjoyed the work and camaraderie of good men.

The Fritzler Place

We made it through our first winter, and spring rolled around again. It was late April 1951. The earth and sky experienced new life too. Weeds poked out of the damp earth. The mosquitoes came out in force. Low spots of the driveway and garden were dry. Geese flew overhead in migration patterns to northern nesting grounds. Robins sang and built nests. Dandelions were everywhere. Spring filled our hearts. It was a glorious time.

Bob and I cleaned up the accumulation of winter debris from the yard and garden. We put the kid's sleds into storage and hung the snow shovels on a wall in the old barn. We washed our hands of winter.

One day, we were resting on a log in the bright, spring sunshine, discussing plans for the upcoming summer work.

"I bet we get kicked off this place," I contemplated.

"Why do you say that?" Bob asked.

"I don't know. I guess I just feel it in my bones."

I was right. About five minutes later, Annie came up behind us and gave us a real scare as she blurted out, "You are too friendly with Herb and

Jewel. You can't be friends with them and me too, so you'll have to move."
She stomped off, ending further debate.

Herb and Jewel lived across the road from Annie, and there had always been bad feelings between them. We were stunned by Annie's abrupt comments. We thought we could be friends with both neighbors.

There was no doubt, as a family, we'd outgrown the little cabin. We'd talked about a larger house, but were content for the time being. Annie had been rude the way she told us to move, so we decided now was as good a time as any to move.

That same day, on our way to Wasilla to pay bills, we noticed an empty house five miles from Annie's cabin. The house and property, known locally as the Fritzler Place, had been sold to the Kitty Neilson and Nils Hanson families, both living in Anchorage. Carl Fritzler gave us Oscar Neilson's address. When we located him, he gave us permission to move in for $50 a month.

In late May 1951, we moved into the house. Kitty, business manager for her family, was Outside in the states visiting. Soon after we moved in, she returned and came out to find us living in her house. She was irate, until she learned Oscar had given us permission to live there. She calmed down and gave us her consent to stay in her house.

The Neilsons had spent many summer hours working on the Fritzler Place, their house in the woods. The house had wide window sills, a perfect place for geraniums, my favorite flower. It had four small rooms with cream-colored walls and bright-red trim. Shiny linoleum added to the cheeriness. The house was completely furnished, clean, and bright. What a blessing! I felt like a new woman in my spacious new home. It had a wonderful, large back porch with shelves from floor to ceiling for storage. There was a large, empty Quonset hut on the property. There was no well, however, and we had to carry water again.

A detached bathroom with a creaky door and breezy ventilation, and it's share of spider webs, was in the back yard. Early the first morning after we moved in, four-year-old Roger, needing to use the biffy, came screaming back to the house.

"Mommy, Mommy, there's a big animal out there, and it's going to get me!"

"Well, come on, show me." I took his tiny hand and there

in the path, was a porcupine, waddling along in his unique way. Roger, so excited, wanted to keep it to show Daddy. We took a wash tub, turned it over the animal, and shared the experience with Daddy that evening before releasing the spiny critter to plod back into the woods.

There were many porcupine in the area then, because there was less cleared land. Kitty Neilson had told us there were strange animals living under the house. We heard loud, grunting noises, but never knew what caused them until one day we saw two porcupine come out from under the house.

Porcupine are slow-moving animals who live on tree bark. They eat up the wooden handle of any tool left lying around, because they crave the salt residue left by humans. Other than being well protected by quills, they're very helpless. We'd heard time after time that porcupine was good to eat. The Holsteins invited us to a roast porcupine dinner one evening. The roast was delicious. I couldn't tell the difference between porcupine and chicken.

The next summer, Bob shot a porcupine, and when the skinning was complete, he came into the house and said to me, "Come out here and tell me what you think."

When I saw the porcupine, I said, "I'm not eating that." He agreed. He never again killed a porcupine, nor did we eat another.

Obtaining electricity was easier than at Annie's cabin; no meter pole to plant or wires to string. The house was wired, but the Neilsons hadn't spent large amounts of time there, so they didn't keep the electric service continually. We made one call, and in a few days, we became customers of Matanuska Electric Association. Simple!

About the time we moved into the Fritzler Place, Bob was through working at the Bureau of Reclamation and was out of work. Along about that time, we met John Lemon, a serious, fair, but short-tempered man we'd become acquainted with at the VFW.

The Road Commission never removed snow from the roads. They simply piled it alongside. Consequently, when the snow melted, the water ran back into the road, creating bogs, sludge, and sticky mud holes lasting far into June. Cars and trucks became mired in this muck.

The day we met John, we couldn't pass his hopelessly stuck truck. Bob got out to help and, eventually, they got John's truck free.

Bob came back to our pickup truck and I said, "Wasn't that John Lemon? Maybe he needs some help at the concrete plant."

John was building sand and gravel bunkers close to Wasilla Lake in preparation for a concrete block business.

"Hey!" said Bob. "Maybe he does." He jumped out of the truck and flagged John down. Luckily, John needed help, and Bob went to work on the following Monday.

Bob didn't get paid regularly, however. John was honest, but with the rigors of operating a new business, he didn't have steady money coming in.

Bob bought a large meat saw while working at the Co-op the first summer. The purchase of a meat saw, and a meat block made of birdseye maple, cost $75.

Bob was anxious to set it up and use it and Ray, our professional meat-cutter friend, went into partnership with him. Along with some charity work for people who didn't have the money to get their meat processed, the men cut meat for hire and were always busy.

Bob had just invested in a used 8N Ford tractor and all the attachments: disc, plow, buzz saw, and a spring tooth harrow. It was a buy for $200 down and $50 a month. With hospital bills for the birth of our daughter, the $1.50 an hour from John was barely enough, especially when it came irregularly. Rent and other payments were due the first of every month. We had to have a steady paycheck to keep afloat.

In July, Bob left John and went to work for MK Construction, building barracks and warehouses on Fort Richardson near Anchorage. In October, severe winter weather shut the job down. Concrete will not setup in temperatures below freezing. Bob had to collect unemployment money for four months, the first and only time in his entire life.

I'd been looking at the empty Quonset hut on the property all summer and winter, and now it seemed ready for a productive venture.

About that same time, I thought of a good use for this lifeless shed—a perfect home for chickens. I decided 100 laying hens would bring the shed to life, keep me busy, and supply us in eggs and meat. Extra eggs could be sold to offset feed bills.

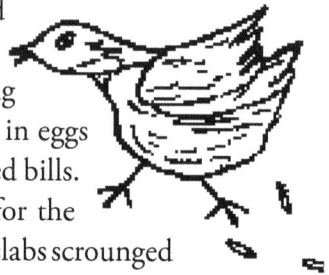

We needed only part of the Quonset hut for the chicks, so Bob partitioned half of it with wood slabs scrounged from a local sawmill. The other half was to be used for storage and, hopefully later, a pen for a breeder sow.

48

Keeping 100 baby chicks warm and fed consumed most of my days and nights for about a month-and-a-half. They devoured sack after sack of chick mash. They soaked up warmth from the heat of an oil-burning brooder stove. The brooder stove is built like a large umbrella close to the floor with a heater in the center. It was fueled with oil from a barrel in the other part of the building. The chicks got under the umbrella to keep warm. The attention this brood demanded kept me busy in many ways I didn't think possible. For a while, it was almost like caring for a new baby. Any sudden movement set the chicks into a panic, causing them to promptly pile up in a corner and suffocate. Keeping the brooder too cold was just as much a catastrophe as keeping it too hot. As the tiny chicks grew to fryer size, they ate themselves out of house and home.

Separating the hens from the roosters was one way to eliminate the number of star boarders. The roosters ended up in the frying pan as Sunday dinner.

By fall, the hens were ready to lay. Bob made nests and roosts for them. We threw straw, and an occasional scoopful of sawdust from our woodpile on the droppings and generously sprinkled it on the floor, to the delight of the chickens. The hens spent a most enjoyable winter singing and scratching in the sawdust and straw, eating mash, and drinking warm water.

They apparently took pleasure from eating snow from our boots so we kept a shovel near the chicken house door. Whenever either one of us entered the hut, we shoveled some snow on top of their litter. This served a double purpose; the hens were happy with this treat and the path to the hut was kept shoveled.

They laid plenty of eggs and were just as content when it was snowing as when it was -20°.

Egg-gathering time soon became a routine chore. A few hens complained loudly with raucous squawks about the invasion of their nests. Some dared me to take eggs from under them by protesting with some well-placed pecks. Friends, neighbors, and the local grocery store bought every egg we could spare.

One day, a friend came to buy some eggs and asked Roger what he was going to be when he grew up. Roger replied, "I'm going to be a Geiger counter." Later, we cleared up his notion and explained that a Geiger was not an animal in the woods.

We constantly culled the hens. After the kids were put to bed for the night, Bob and I, with a gunny sack and flashlight, quietly and cautiously made our way to the hen house. Bob measured the distance between the hen's pelvic bones—two fingers wide was an indication of a good layer.

As we plucked each hen from the roost, it squawked until it was gently replaced. Two chickens at each culling session were all I could dress out. At times, we checked as many as 12 hens before finding two that we considered culls.

During one of our culling sessions, I offered our neighbor, Delores Levan, a deal she couldn't refuse.

"If you come over and help me dress out some fryers tomorrow, you can take two home for dinner," I offered.

Delores willingly accepted. Early the following morning, we tackled the job of dressing out six fryers.

With her four children and my two, we divided our time between settling kid's fights and dressing out fryers.

That same afternoon, with two live roosters in a gunny sack, Delores and her four young ones went home happy with their prize.

A few days later, when stopping by the Levan homestead on the way to the grocery store in Wasilla, she greeted us at her door. Delores excitedly told us, "I thought you gave me two roosters. Yesterday ,when I butchered them, I found what looked like eggs in them."

Grinning broadly from ear to ear, Bob exclaimed, "Those were roosters all right. Were there two eggs in each?"

Then it dawned on her what the two so called eggs were. Her face turned beet-red and, to avoid anymore undue embarrassment, she quickly changed the subject and invited us into her home for a cup of coffee and cinnamon rolls fresh out of the oven.

Our chicken venture lasted two years. During that time, I met many people who came for fresh eggs. Their visits were a welcome change from caring for the babies all day and not seeing adults. I got the valley news and made some pocket money too.

We never tired of custards, french toast, deviled eggs, angel food cakes, and homemade ice cream. I fried, roasted, or stewed chickens, and I also canned some for use in chicken and dumplings. We sold some chickens as stewing hens.

About the same time, we decided to raise turkeys. We purchased six baby turkeys from the Matanuska Valley Farmers Cooperative Association in Palmer. The first month, we kept them in a large cardboard box in the corner of the kitchen. Using what we had, and improvising with the need to keep the birds warm, Bob fixed up a Rube Golberg electric light.

At first, they wouldn't eat. A friend said to put some bright colored marbles in their feed. Turkeys are attracted to bright colors and will unconsciously peck at them until they learn there's food around the marbles. We used newspapers and sawdust for their bedding, but, as they grew, the odor became more and more unbearable, even with daily changing. This forced us to move them to the Quonset hut. During the warmest part of the day, we'd let them feed on the new grass in the yard.

Shortly after we moved into the Fritzler Place, we spent $100 from the sale of the travel trailer on a full-grown female, Chester White pig. We hoped to breed her and sell enough little weaner pigs at $15 each to pay the cost of purchasing the sow.

We built a pen in the other half of the Quonset hut. Bob brought her home in the back of our pickup truck, unloaded her and tried to get her into her new home. She went halfway, balked, perched herself calmly on top of a small mound of sawdust, and surveyed her new surroundings. Roger and I were watching from the cabin porch.

"What shall we name the pig?" I asked five-year-old Roger.

"Sawdust!" he exclaimed. And Sawdust she was.

Sawdust was content in the Quonset hut until summer. Then Bob built her a little house and enclosed an area for exercise and feeding with a sturdy fence made of thick slabs of wood left from the chicken project.

At breeding time, Bob and Ralph tried every way to get Sawdust, whose head seemed on the wrong end, into the truck bed. Swearing, sweating, and disgruntled, they tried to think of some new way to get 200 pounds of pig into a truck.

I watched their antics and finally edged my way in and said, "Here, let me try." I had some of her favorite grain and when she got her greedy nose well into my bucket, I backed slowly into the truck with her following me. She was locked in before she realized she'd been tricked. The men, speechless that it looked so simple, got into the truck and took her to a 'hog friend' for breeding.

Early the following spring, the sow gave birth to 12 pink piglets. As the weather moderated and browse for the pigs became nonexistent, we put a low-electric fence around a large area for the pigs to exercise and root to their heart's content. The fence was only six inches off the ground, but the pigs had great respect for it. We sold 11 piglets as six-week-old weaner pigs, and got back more than our original $100.

Before the weaner pigs were sold, Bob castrated the males. He'd often watched his father do this. He had the knowledge and confidence to do the job, although this was the first time he'd attempted it on his own with our livestock.

On the morning Bob was to do the castrating, he stepped over the electric fence and grabbed one of the piglets. It squealed, but Bob didn't pay much attention and proceeded to the Quonset hut. I was watching all this from the house porch and saw Sawdust running after him with her mouth wide open. The electric fence did not slow her down.

"Bob, Sawdust is right behind you. Run!" I yelled.

Bob kept a firm hold on the piglet and managed to slide into the Quonset hut and slam the door shut before the sow got close.

The sow was running around the yard, confused and disoriented. When she was some distance from the hut, I left Roger in the cabin and ran to the hut to help Bob.

Bob put a gunny sack on a upside down, 50-gallon barrel, turned the pig over on its back and operated as I held its legs. When the first piglet was castrated, Bob turned it loose, the sow reclaimed it, and both were herded into the pig house and locked in while we worked on the other male piglets. The only antiseptic used was lard and kerosene. None of the piglets experienced any complications.

One day, while the kids and I were at Delores' house visiting, Bob drove into our yard and heard a blood-curdling screech coming from the pigpen. Sawdust and the piglets were terrified of a big black bear hanging over the fence. Pigs have an inordinate fear and hatred for bear and raise an alarm when one is in the vicinity. The noise of the pickup must have frightened the bear away, because we never saw it again. When we abandoned the garden for the summer, the pigs were allowed to roam at will. They made themselves a nest of hay, leaves, and twigs on the sunny south side of the house.

One day, Roger was looking out the window, saw the piglets, all in a line, hopping on one another demonstrating biological urges. He said, "Look, Mommy, the pigs are playing train." I had to leave the room so I could giggle out loud.

We were in town one day and the pigs decided to do a little exploring on their own. The door of the porch wasn't securely fastened, and the pigs made their way inside. They wrecked havoc with everything within their reach, including several old pillows stored on low shelves. When we entered the porch later that day, we were greeted by a swirling cloud of feathers. Everything else in the porch was ransacked into an enormous mess.

In 1952, on a February day, driving from the library where Roger and I had spent the afternoon, a moose dashed from the woods near our home. The truck slid on the icy road as I slammed on the brakes trying to avoid the animal. We struck the moose. He crashed over the hood into the windshield, then bounced into the ditch. Roger, standing up in the truck, nearly got kicked in the face. We were both terrified. I leaned on the horn as I continued to the house.

Bob came out and assessed the damage. He could see we weren't hurt, so he wasn't too upset and left for work. On his way to work, Bob stopped and reported the incident to the Commissioner in Wasilla. The moose, with a broken back, was lying beside the road. Commissioner May Carter's husband, Pat, and Jim Kennedy, a friend of his, left immediately for the site. They shot, and dressed out the moose and donated the meat to the Wasilla School lunch program. Wild game was legal to use in school menus.

Weeks later, we saw Pat in Wasilla. He jokingly teased us about the moose having no liver or tenderloin. I thought about it for a long time. Bob and I finally figured out Pat and Jim kept the liver and tenderloin—the choice parts of a young bull moose.

The Buffalo Coal Mine, near Sutton, hired Bob to fire boilers. He enjoyed this job, and it paid well. The mine was owned by Mr. Nesbitt, an Anchorage lawyer, who later became the Chief Justice of Alaska Superior Court. Bob worked from 4 PM to midnight for about five months. He still talks about his fascination with the aurora borealis, or northern lights. Their twisting, darting patterns of red, blue, and green moving bands of color and their swishing sounds are formed from solar rays refracting light through space particles. Often he'd stop his truck on the way home, stand in the darkness, and enjoy the display.

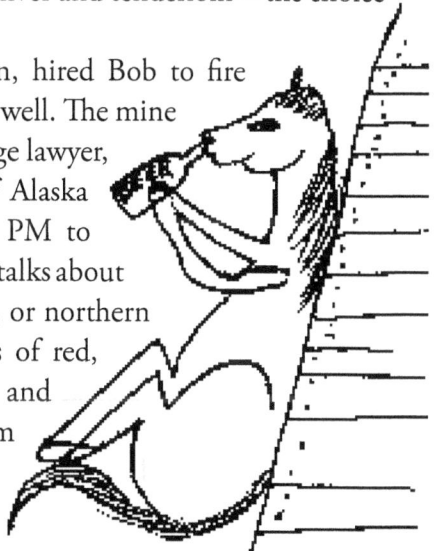

Bob heard about Wiggins' Construction Company hiring men to build a telephone line from Anchorage to Tok Junction. Bob started out as a carpenter's helper. One day, the low-boy driver quit and Bob got the job. The wages for this job were much better than the wages for a laborer. Some days, he made $60, including overtime. That was big money in those days.

While Bob was in the Marines, he'd had no trouble backing a semi-truck next to a building or into a parking lot. Backing a semi-truck off unimproved roads, between trees, and through mud was another story. The only time Bob could use a low-boy truck to move a D-2 tractor was at night, after the crew was off work, the day boss had gone home, and everyone was out of his way. His work shift stretched all day and into early evening.

A white horse belonging to one of the lodges hung around camp when they were working in the Sheep Mountain area. The men fed it beer. The horse would allow the men to put the bottle in his mouth, then he'd raise his head, guzzle the beer and look around for more. After consuming a couple of beers, he'd get to feeling good, lay down, and sleep it off. This was entertainment for the men every evening; that is, for those who were not playing poker, gambling, or drinking beer themselves.

The men didn't come home every weekend because it was 200 miles, one way. They moved camp every two weeks to keep up with the telephone line. Bob managed to come home once in a while, but after six weeks, he quit. He wanted to entertain his parents who were making their first trip to our Alaska home. Bob's father liked Alaska right away and told us it reminded him of Canada when he homesteaded there in 1908. While visiting, his dad babied a runt calf and put it in good shape. He fed it cut potatoes and turnips, and he watered it several times a day.

I was unhappy with Bob's decision to quit, because if he had worked another six weeks, until freeze-up, we could have paid off some bills and built up our savings account. Back then if a job ended, or you were laid off, in October when Termination Dust covered the Talkeetna Mountains, you could count on being out of work until spring melted the snow.

One day, when our family was visiting the Levan homestead, Delores told us about her five-year-old son, John. The curious youngster had found a can of lye stored under the kitchen sink and accidently rubbed some into his eye. Damage was severe. The doctor ordered an immediate operation to remove his eye. When John came home from the hospital, he was his usual, mischievous self. A glass eye replaced his damaged eye. This was quite a novelty to the five-year-old.

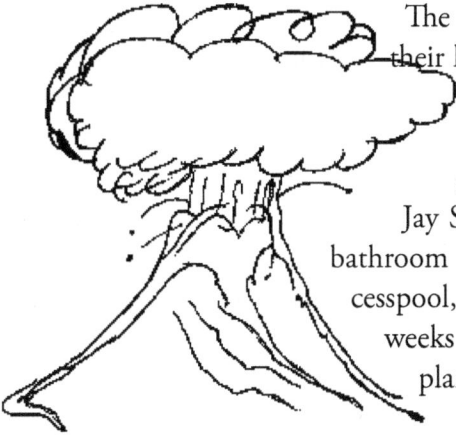

The Levans had a flush toilet installed in their home during John's hospital stay. He was intrigued with the flush toilet. His greatest delight was to take out his glass eye and flush it down the toilet. Jay Sr., his father, plumbed most of the bathroom during his free time. He built the cesspool, and it was in working order for weeks before he could get it covered with planking and soil.

Whenever John came out of the bathroom without his glass eye, Delores shouted to their five-year-old son, Jay, "Go out to the cesspool and get John's eye."

Jay complied to her demand willingly. In fact, he enjoyed it. Jay Sr. had contrived a long-handled dipper out of an old tin can punched with holes and nailed to a narrow board about six feet long. Jay loved to use this scoop to find the glass eye floating on top of the cesspool. Delores began locking the bathroom door and wouldn't let John in unless accompanied by her or Jay.

Life at our place was filled with humor, like the story of little John Levan's glass eye. Stories like this still make us chuckle.

On July 3, 1953, Bob was driving to Anchorage on a delivery run. He got as far as Allen's Grocery, in Chugiak, when he saw a black cloud in a dark sky, coming from the southwest. Someone in the store said it looked like rain. Bob said it looked like a volcanic eruption. Everyone in the store laughed at him in disbelief. He kept the radio playing in his pickup and, sure enough, a news report said Mount Spur was erupting. When he got to Anchorage, it was pitch dark from falling ash. He could hardly see lights across the street, even though it was noon. Three hours later, there was three inches of ash blanketing Anchorage. Car paint was pitted, engines ruined, and airplanes grounded. Bob came home safely and bragged about being right about the volcano erupting.

The valley experienced very little fallout. Bob noticed pit marks in the paint of his new pickup, and I brushed a light sprinkling of ash from my garden plants.

The following day, Bob took Roger, who

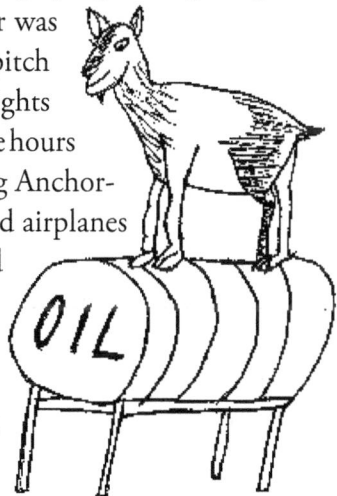

was seven, to Anchorage to see the damage. On another delivery route, Roger, the entrepreneur, told Bob he should gather the ash into bottles. They gathered three bottles of ash and later donated two bottles to a school science display. Since then, we've been offered $25 for the last bottle of ash.

With two kids and another on the way, we decided we needed a supply of fresh milk. A cow was too expensive to maintain, so after much discussion, we decided a goat was a good idea.

We drove to a farm near Palmer and talked to a man named Johnnie about a goat. Johnnie lived alone on his farm, without a wife to protest about the dump he called home. He never cleaned anything. He slept in a sleeping bag until it was filthy. He never washed dishes, windows or floors. Garbage filled the front yard; everything from broken parts to trash. He was slovenly in his dress, too, and seldom took a bath. Everyone who got within sniffing distance could tell. He smelled like the goats he let into his house. They licked his plates clean and drank from his water bucket. It wasn't any wonder his wife had been sent to Morningside Mental Hospital in Oregon, for a long rest.

He finally took our $20, shoved it into his pocket, and gave us pointers on caring for and feeding the goat.

If we'd let the goat run free, our garden would have been in shambles. After we tied her, if there was a stick or twig on the ground anywhere near her stake, she'd manage to become hopelessly entangled. I came to her rescue to unsnarl her twisted chain many times.

Bob finally made an enclosure for her, but she climbed out anyway by walking up the boards used to brace the fence. She loved human companionship. At mealtimes, she'd jump onto the oil barrels located under our dining room window, chew her cud, shake her whiskers and watch us eat. If she wasn't amused by the family meals, she'd climb onto the cab of the pickup truck parked near the dining room window and bleat at us in protest.

We tried everything to keep her inside a fenced yard, but to no avail. After two months of putting up with her antics, Bob announced he was going to return the troublesome goat to Johnnie.

"Why? I assumed the goat's milk idea was a good one," I stated.

"Because she's smarter than I am, that's why!" Bob retorted.

As I swept the goat raisins from the front steps, Bob loaded the goat into the truck for her trip back to Johnnie's farm.

Johnnie was the local Watkins Product dealer and lacked money to buy the goat back. We accepted $20 worth of Watkins Products in exchange. I had soap and vanilla for many years.

One day, Johnnie came to our house peddling his Watkins Products. During his discussion, he mentioned his church was having a social that evening and invited Bob and me. I informed Johnnie that Bob worked nights and it was impossible for us to attend. Johnnie quickly told me he'd be most happy to escort me. I teased Bob that I couldn't have been in too bad of shape for being nine months pregnant, because a man still asked me for a date.

On February 15,1954, we took the kids to the Lemon's home, then Bob drove me to Palmer Hospital. The next morning, Linda Jo was born. She was the biggest baby of our three kids—eight pounds seven ounces, brown hair and blue eyes. Roger thought she was special and Barbara was sure Linda belonged to her. Now there were five of us in the house.

A few days before Linda was born, a box containing used baby clothes was given to me. When Barbara was a baby, I had donated clothes to the box for other expectant mothers in the community. When Linda was born, I received the box back. It was fun to go through it and see and use Barbara's old clothes for Linda. When I was through using them, I passed the box on to someone else in need. This box of clothes was as good as any of today's baby showers. All I had to buy was a few diapers, undershirts, and an up-town blanket, one I would use exclusively for going to town or church. We appreciated the baby clothes and took good care of them for the next person.

During the previous months, Palmer Hospital had been under construction and Linda was to be the first baby born in the new hospital, entitling her to gifts and local publicity. Construction was delayed three months and the hospital wasn't dedicated until May 16th, three months after Linda's birth. I was disappointed about the delay but have been able to tell the exact date of the dedication of the hospital to anyone who asked.

From the spring of 1953, to the summer of 1954, Bob worked with Wayne Hunter as partners in a delivery service between Anchorage and Valley points. They decided Wayne would write the company's checks, Bob would make deliveries on certain routes, and Wayne would take the others. They each had a new, blue, 1/2-ton pickup, with leather upholstery and other extras, bought by the company. They took orders from Sutton to Eagle River, picked them up in Anchorage, and delivered them in the evening on the way back to Wasilla.

They delivered the daily newspaper and freight to lodges, restaurants, and grocery stores. In those days, the road to Anchorage was much longer because it went from Palmer, across the Knik River, along the mountains and past the Eklutna power plant. The road was gravel all the way. It was dusty in summer, slick in winter, and tolerable in between. Snow slides and flooding were a common occurrence. Sometimes, there were no bridges in places and it was necessary to drive across the streams on portable Army Bailey bridges.

Occasionally Roger, age seven, and Barbara, age three, accompanied Bob. What a fun day it would be for them. They'd drive out of the yard, smiling and happy. I'd think to myself, "Goody, goody. I have the day all to myself. Just baby Linda and me, and no lunch to fix."

They left early in the morning and got home about 6 PM. The lodges along the way gave the kids treats. The Anchorage Times gave them leftovers from newsprint rolls. They spent many hours on rainy days, drawing and coloring on this paper. Gilman's Bakery gave them jelly rolls. I could tell because the kids had jelly on their faces when they got home. They admired the graders and bulldozers at Northern Commercial Company and the airplanes at Merrill Field.

Bob started delivering newspapers and became very skilled at tossing them into driveways. Keeping a tight focus on his driving, and as accurate as any hunter, with his eye never leaving his target, he'd quickly grab a newspaper from his bag, and in one graceful motion, heave it through the truck window. With a snap of his wrist, he sent the paper hurtling over the top of the cab. The paper glided in the air, end over end, until it skidded to a halt. Seldom did he miss the driveway. The kids were awed by his skill and wanted to imitate him. Bob accommodated them by driving closer to the mail boxes to aid their accuracy

Bob also sold our excess garden produce to patrons along his route. Our carrots were huge. A lady in Sutton couldn't believe they were garden variety and accused Bob of peddling horse carrots. Horse carrots are a species of carrot, extra large and fibrous, raised in the Lower-48, for animal feed.

After getting a letter from Inlet Motors about being several months delinquent on truck payments, Bob told the officials there to hold the check and he'd call them when it was good. Bob knew that Wayne procrastinated in making bank deposits. A few days later, Wayne made a sizeable deposit, so Bob called Inlet Motors. They immediately cashed the rubber check. Bob never told Wayne what he'd done. When Wayne found out he was livid. Bob legally dissolved the partnership in June 1954.

During the three years we lived on the Fritzler Place, we were on the lookout for a homestead. We asked questions of everyone and were told the best land was already taken. Harold Harris told of a homestead close to his. A soldier named Donald Fox had filed on the land, but abandoned it when he was discharged from the Army at Fort Richardson, and returned to Missouri to live. Bob wrote him a letter contesting ownership of his homestead. Mr. Fox wrote back and was eager to relinquish homestead rights to the land.

Bob sent the necessary papers to him and Mr. Fox signed them. Next, Bob sent filing and relinquishment papers to the land office in Anchorage. We could take possession of our land at anytime within six months. By law, as veterans of WWII, we could homestead 160 acres by building a habitable house and living on the acreage for seven months. A non-veteran was required to build his house, cultivate 1/8 of his ground and live on the premises for three years.

The homestead was now ours! I immediately thought of the great challenge for myself and my family. I knew in my heart that, even though we didn't know about homesteading, if we took it one day at a time, we could make it all we wanted it to be.

Jim Kennedy, an old-timer from Wasilla, visited often in our home and regaled us with tales of the old days in Washington and Oregon; of being a professional horse thief; of smuggling liquor during prohibition days. His stories entertained us, and our kids thought he was a real Jesse James. He told us he went straight when telephones came into general use between towns. We never knew him to be dishonest or doing disservice to anyone. Jim suggested building our homestead house from the plentiful trees in the region. He told us he owned a sawmill that we could set up on our place to cut the trees into three-sided logs.

During the spring, Jim and Bob set up the sawmill on the Fritzler Place. Good stands of spruce and cottonwood were available. This convinced us to build a log house on our homestead. The mill squared off the logs on three sides, for ease in building. Each time we took a trip to the homestead, we hauled a few logs and stacked them near our building site. It took all summer.

About the time Jim and Bob began working with the sawmill, we bought seven turkeys. Several times, the men noticed two malamute dogs eyeing the turkeys from the edge of the woods. They were big working dogs that

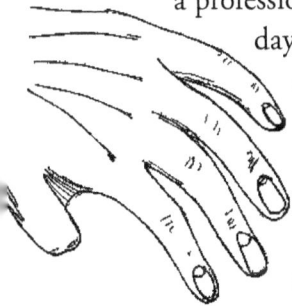

loved to roam free. Often, they turned wild again and became a nuisance. The men could tell the dogs were anticipating a free meal. Bob took his rifle with him the next few days and leaned it against the Quonset hut within easy reach. Soon, he got the opportunity to eliminate the two problems. Jim kept saying, "I didn't see a thing. I didn't see a thing."

While Bob was working days in the delivery business, he helped Jim on the sawmill at night, on weekends, and sometimes early in the morning. Bob was always tired from lack of sleep and from working too hard.

One day, the sawdust conveyor quit working. Jim left the saw running and went to take care of the conveyor problem. While waiting for Jim to return, Bob laid his right hand on the thick log being sawed. Only 1/2 inch of the saw blade was visible. When he leaned on his hand, the whirring blade grabbed the glove on his hand and cut off his thumb. All that remained attached was a blood vessel keeping the thumb and hand together.

As the empty glove sailed past Jim, he had visions of Bob's hand still in it. Jim immediately shut down the mill and both men raced to the house. I used a clean diaper, the best compress I could find, on his hand, and gave Jim instructions to stay with the kids. With Bob in a state of shock, I madly drove the truck toward Palmer Hospital. At one point, I didn't think I'd make it, for a teen-aged girl was nonchalantly herding cattle alongside the road. She didn't hurry the beasts. Even my frantic honking didn't help.

Dr. Bailey gave Bob a shot to put him out, and then he sewed the thumb back. Bob spent two weeks in the hospital, and I managed with three small kids as best I could.

Bob was glad to be home out of the hospital to good farmer food. Two weeks later, during an office visit, Dr. Bailey pretended to look at Bob's thumb, gave a quick jerk, and pulled the pin out.

"Why didn't you warn me you were going to pull the pin?" Bob winced. "It hurt like hell!"

"If I had, you couldn't have stood the pain. Now it's done, and I'm sure it'll heal nicely." Doctor Bailey quickly cleaned his hands and left the room.

We had to be living on the homestead by August 1954. Because of Bob's accident, we couldn't meet the deadline, so we were granted a 30-day extension by the Land Office. By September, the site for the house was dozed off to gravel, leveled, and graded. Work on our home could begin.

Udder Confusion

For several weeks, we went back and forth from our rented house to the homestead to work on our new log home. Bob worked most days taking care of a 30-acre potato field that he and Harold Harris were jointly farming. In the evening, when Bob came home from work, we'd take care of chores at the rented house, then drive to the homestead and put in a few hours of labor on our new palace.

Bob taught me how to use a draw knife. I'd peel two or more logs Bob positioned on saw horses, while he kept busy at other tasks. The kids kept themselves amused playing and exploring around the building site. The logs I'd finish were settled firmly into place and two new logs were put onto saw horses and I'd repeat the task the next night. Bit by bit, like worker bees, we raised three courses of logs.

Bob and I used no modern tools. We didn't have electricity, so Bob used a level, hammer, carpenter's square, and draw knife. He drove 10-inch spikes with a sledge hammer and staggered them along the log to prevent splitting. He drilled through the top log and halfway through the bottom log to countersink the spikes. He used a crosscut saw to square off the ends. He used an axe to cut notches in the log ends, so the top log would fit over the log below. Spikes cost $30 a keg. I recall thinking $30 was a lot of money.

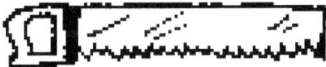

Progress on the log house was slow because Bob's right hand was in a cast after badly cutting his thumb at the saw mill. He learned how to pound nails with his left hand and became very proficient. We worked as a team. I held the nail until he got it started in the wood. Then he finished pounding it home. Some time later, when the cast was taken off his right hand, Bob was astonished that he was better at pounding nails with his left hand. He's since lost that ability. He lost 20 pounds trying to raise potatoes, a financial disaster, and also build a house.

As the weather settled down to winter, snow appeared on mountain peaks and ice formed in water puddles. With the onset of colder weather, we were faced with a dilemma. Our new house was nowhere near completion. It had four short walls. We were running out of time. We decided to build a small shanty on the sub-floor, 12- by 18-feet, which was the size of our future kitchen. We did so by completing two of the short walls to eight feet. We then enclosed the shanty by building two temporary stud walls. These temporary outside walls of the shanty would later serve as a partition of the living room, bathroom, and kitchen of the completed house.

We'd live in the shanty until we built the two remaining log walls around us. We moved into our shanty late in September, 1954, with three small kids. Roger was seven, Barbara was four and Linda was seven months. We borrowed a small travel trailer from Jim Kennedy and moved it to the homestead, close to the foundation, and used it for sleeping quarters for Roger and Barbara.

Our shanty held a crib, a double bed, a table and four chairs, and the large combination electric stove we bought while we were in the cabin at Annie's. Wooden boxes nailed to the walls served as cupboards. Toys, food, clothes, and other supplies were stored under beds. We kept most of our household goods, including Bob's tools, in boxes in other portions of the unfinished building. Snug in our shanty, we plodded onward to complete the other two remaining walls.

With winter snowfalls ready to swoop down upon us, it became obvious we weren't going to get the house closed in. Friends donated two day's labor to complete the walls. John Lemon assisted with the roof, a two -day task. Bob boarded up all the windows except one in the front and one in the back of the house.

We connected electricity in December, then dismantled the shack, board by board. Bob took the back window of the house out of the frame and threw the boards into a heap near the house. We hurriedly put the window back in place, expanded our living quarters into the whole house, then settled down to a long winter of trying to keep warm.

Once the house was enclosed, we spent the rest of the winter, as time and money dictated, insulating and finishing the inside. Every extra minute I had, I chinked logs on the inside of the house with oakum, a hemp rope soaked in oil. Green logs have a tendency to twist as they dry; chinking filled any gaps. In December, it plunged to a bitter -20. Since the house was totally enclosing the shanty, we installed a barrel stove in the living room. Every homestead had one. A barrel stove was an empty 50-gallon gasoline drum laid on its side, set on legs, with a hole cut into one end and a door attached. A hole cut into the top of the other end was for the smoke stack. These stoves were easily acquired and cheap to make, but were temperamental. Sometimes, they'd roar and turn red from the heat of a good fire, but sometimes, no matter what was done, they refused to hold a fire.

Bob cut wood by the cord, even when it was -20. To this day, he believes cutting wood gave his thumb the proper circulation that it needed in order to heal as nicely as it did. That winter he also milked a family cow by hand, which greatly helped him in getting strength back in his thumb.

The fall after we moved onto the homestead, Bob took time out from building on the house to erect a small barn to shelter the family Jersey cow, named Melanie and a calf we called Petunia. Eight-year-old Roger learned how to milk Melanie.

During February, we had a lot of rain, and slippery ice coated everything. Melanie fell on the ice and couldn't get up. When we found her, she was stranded on her belly, her legs were splayed, and her udder was in contact with the ice. It was several hours before we were able to get her up again. She was ruined, her hips strained and her udder frozen. We had no choice but to destroy her. We were saddened, but accidents like this do happen on the farm.

When we moved to our homestead we brought the young. In the fall, as time permitted, Bob hand-dug a well near the house. He put a brace between the branches of two trees near the house and hung a pulley to winch buckets of dirt from the well. The turkeys soon discovered that this bracing was an ideal spot to roost for the night. The nights were now getting cooler, and the turkeys huddled closer and

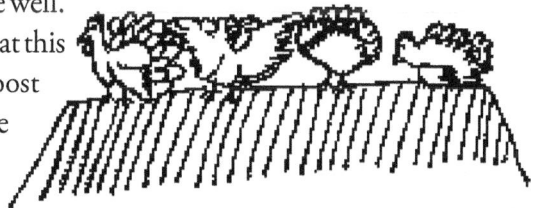

closer to each other, eventually crowding each other into the well. At daylight the ruckus of the turkeys trying to get out of the well had started. It was the beginning of a new day for the turkeys and for Bob. He'd drag himself out of bed, dress, pull on his boots and jacket, curse every inch of the way, climb down the ladder and retrieve them, one by one, from the well. Ungratefully, they fought him claw and wing.

We didn't need an alarm clock, for early each morning, the turkeys which hadn't fallen in the well, climbed from the brace to the shanty roof. The clump, clump of their long spurs walking across the tar-paper roof of our shanty made a most obnoxious noise, enough so we knew sleeping was useless.

One large, tom turkey was mean. We were saving him for an upcoming holiday meal, but plans changed. Barbara was walking across the yard toward the house when the tom turkey came up behind her, flew onto her shoulders. He began beating her with his wings, and pecking her on the head. She ran, screamed, and flailed her arms at the assailant. Bob, working nearby, grabbed the axe, chased the turkey away from Barbara, caught it, and chopped it's head off, right then and there. One less turkey for the holidays. He hugged Barbara and told her everything was OK.

Just before Thanksgiving, we dressed out the turkeys. No store-bought turkey was ever as tender or tasty as those turkeys.

Winters on the homestead were long, cold, and dark. There weren't many open fields. The forest closed in on the small houses and cabins. Their distant, twinkling lights through the trees assured warmth.

We consumed enormous amounts of time carrying water for household use and getting enough wood cut ahead for the stoves. After a deep snow-fall, the roads would drift shut as strong winds blew the snow around. At times, we waited four days for roads to be cleared.

Winds blew from the north east, off the Matanuska Glacier and into the Matanuska Valley during the winter. Gusts from 60 to 100 miles per hour were possible. Fields and open spaces were left bare. Fierce cold winds could blow two to four days at a time. Unprotected skin could freeze in seven seconds. Drifted roads and terrible chill factors would close the schools.

After one blow, I phoned and complained to the Road Commission. It seemed like we were always last to have our road cleared. The receptionist said, "Well, somebody has to be last." I was left entirely speechless.

During our wood-burning days, after routine chores were finished, we spent any spare time cutting wood. Bob and Roger drove the tractor into the nearby woods to find trees. The further they went into the woods, the more they risked getting stuck in drifted snow or low spots, so they stayed close to home. Bob was in charge of the chain saw; Roger trimmed the limbs with an axe and stacked brush.

Moose in our area soon learned to recognize the chain saw noise. While a tree was being trimmed on the stump end, moose were feeding on the top branches. Roger deliberately left them a pile of branches, brush, and twigs. They both used extreme caution, for moose could be dangerous when hungry. By February or March, moose had a difficult time finding browse. Moose require about 25 pounds dry weight of browse a day to stay healthy. With deep snow covering the low brush, it was common to find moose starved to death.

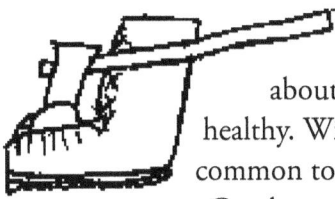

Good, warm clothes were not available in those days, so we wore extra pairs of warm socks inside leather boots. Long-johns and an extra shirt or sweater helped to repel the cold.

One winter Bob bought himself a new pair of insulated leather boots. The first day he wore them, he spent an hour splitting wood. Evidently he hit a knot in the wood, the axe glanced off and hit the toe of his new boot, slashing a three inch cut. Though his foot was not injured, he complained of one warm foot and one cold foot the rest of the winter. No matter how much sympathy I gave him, it didn't give him two warm feet.

All farm chores had to be done, regardless of weather conditions. Keeping plumbing from freezing was a never-ending responsibility. I worried about Bob and Roger getting chilled to the bone. Any time they came in from their chores, I tried to have a cup of hot chocolate or a bowl of steaming soup waiting.

As we rested in bed at night, we could hear the wind howling and roaring through the trees and across the roof like a locomotive. The sheet-metal roof would rattle and boom like marbles in a tin can. "No use worrying about losing life or limb." Bob always said, "If you were born to hang, you weren't going to drown." He then used the calm daylight hours to assess damage and set things in order.

Many times, if the wind wasn't too strong, the kids took their sleds and let the wind push them down the icy road in front of our house. Generally, there was no traffic as long as the wind blew.

I accepted winter winds as part of the season, but hated the wintery blasts. I looked forward to balmy spring breezes and summer rain.

"All work and no play makes Jack a dull boy!" also applied to our family. Entertainment consisted mostly of activities we could enjoy for free, or for very little money.

Movies in Palmer were a rare treat. Before the movie started, we purchased ice cream cones at Bert's Drug Store, across the street from the movie house.

The VFW held their annual picnic on the 4th of July every year. They invited all the kids from the community to free hot dogs and ice cream cones. Of course, hordes of kids showed up. I helped dispense the ice cream cones, and I know many kids who came had these treats only at this once-a-year event.

Races and games were held for the kids, and a baseball game was the highlight of the day. By 5 PM, we drove three tired, dirty, but happy, kids home.

When Barbara was about six, we drove home without her. Since it was a beautiful day, the kids rode in the back of the pickup . When we arrived home Bob said, "Where's Barbara?" The other two kids said they thought she was with us in the front of the pickup. We raced back to Wasilla to retrieve our forgotten daughter. We found her standing in the middle of the ball field, seemingly very content and in no danger.

I said to her, "Why aren't you upset about us leaving you here?"

She just smiled and said, "I knew you'd be back to get me."

Probably the big event of the year was the Follies, a local talent show open to anyone. Everyone attended the packed performances held for two nights. Musical numbers and skits were dramatized by neighbors and friends.

The most popular act was the men's cancan line. The dancers wore suits, slacks, dresses, overalls, or work clothes. Local bachelors enjoyed being in this act. It was amazing how much talent was hidden in the Wasilla woods.

One act, which was particularly enjoyed by all, was performed by a lady who walked onto the stage between acts dressed in a different costume each time; for instance, a dancer, a model, a tennis player, or a school teacher. As she paraded across the stage in front of the curtain, she asked the audience, "Anyone?"

No response.

The last time she paraded across the stage in a scanty nightgown and again said, "Anyone?"

The audience rocked the room with peels of laughter.

This March event made a great contribution to breaking up the winter doldrums.

Occasionally, various organizations showed old movies at the school

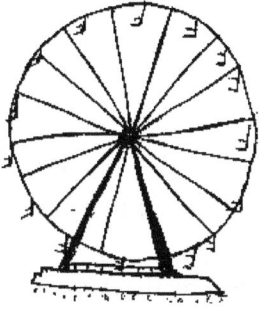

on weekends for 25 cents a ticket. These organizations used the proceeds to bolster their dire financial circumstances. The annual teacher's play was also popular. The local teachers acted out a play to raise money for the PTA. The high school play was another well-attended event.

The Alaska State Fair in Palmer was the grand event of summer. It was always held over Labor Day weekend and was the final big fling before school started. We attended the fair as a family, and as the kids got older, they went their separate ways, always meeting at a predetermined time at the fairground main entrance.

The kids had to make serious decisions at the fair, about how to spend part of their hard-earned summer wages. A hot dog and cotton candy was first on the list. They spent any remaining money on rides, of which the Ferris wheel was a favorite.

The midway games beckoned them also, but they soon learned that the hucksters were at the winning end of the stick.

Since they were active in the local 4H club, they spent a lot of time in the 4H building, seeing who won ribbons and which displays their competitors entered.

Fair time was also an opportunity to see friends we hadn't seen since the last fair. At the end of a long, exhausting day, we were all ready to go home and tumble into bed.

For several years, I was hired to work at the fair. I worked at the main gate selling tickets. I remember being responsible for $8,000 collected at the end of my shift. I also spent a few years "baby-sitting" the canned and baked goods. I thoroughly enjoyed this lucrative stint, just before I had to go to work on the farm. By this time the last of the garden produce was ready for the freezer and the potatoes were ready to be dug.

One winter during the 1950s, we spent Saturday nights at the basement-home of our friends, the Carr family. We were all going to learn how to dance. Neighbors and friends from the immediate area came, laden with favorite treats and a determination to learn every new dance LeRoi Heaven, our able dance instructor, could teach.

Children of all ages danced with each other or with parents. We pushed furniture aside to make room for the dances, ranging from square to ballroom and everything in between.

After midnight, the Carr's served refreshments and then the tired, weary dancers made their way home. Some of us weren't the most graceful of dancers, but the fun was in the camaraderie and togetherness we all enjoyed.

We also made our own entertainment at home. We played 20 questions, card games, and checkers, and listened to the radio. We made popcorn and candy, and read books and magazines from the library.

In due time, we bought a television. We didn't use it until after the evening chores were done. Besides that, programs were only broadcast from six to 11 PM. With the advent of the TV, visiting friends and neighbors gradually disappeared. We never had to lock our doors, during the homestead years. We never worried about vandalism or theft.

In the summer, we made ice cream with our own eggs, milk and cream. I filled empty coffee cans with water, and put them in the freezer to make ice. In the winter, the kids broke icicles from the house eaves, put them in a gunny sack, and pounded the sack with a hammer until it was crushed enough to churn ice cream.

One of the other popular things the teenagers did was go ice skating and have marshmallow roasts after school. The kids took snow shovels and cleared off a place on Lake Lucille or Wasilla Lake, both within walking distance of the school. They gathered wood and built a fire on the shore. In those days, skating didn't cost anything. People have spent millions of dollars today building ice skating rinks. Sometimes, I feel kids today don't know how to make their own fun. Kids were encouraged to be creative or there wasn't any fun.

In December 1954, Bob went to work at the Alaska Experimental Farm, located half-way between Palmer and Wasilla. The pay was $1.50 an hour for taking care of the livestock and other assigned duties. When planting time came, he seeded oats and peas for silage and other grains for thrashing. Bob learned a lot about farming while working there. He became quite knowledgeable about fertilizers and said it took some time to get the formulas through his head. He learned that 100 acres of cleared, usable land is needed to feed 30 cows, our dream of a working Grade A dairy.

Bob worked with the livestock; pigs, poultry, and cattle. The bulls on the Experimental Farm were a ton of ornery power—mean and dangerous. When taken to and from the exercise yard, a one-inch lead rope was snapped into their nose ring and run through a pulley between pen and yard. If a bull ever got loose, it would be almost impossible to capture it again, and then only with a tranquilizer gun. The bulls were breeding stock for artificial insemination.

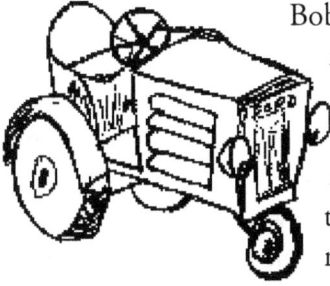

Bob took his lunch from home, as most of the men who worked there did. They'd congregate during lunch hour and talk politics, gossip, nit-pick, etc. One day, it was pick on Gene day. Gene, rather gullible and easy to tease, told the crew that Joe, a friend of his, hadn't returned a borrowed tractor.

"Winter's coming and I need that tractor and he hasn't even mentioned it," he whined.

Earl, a practical joker said, munching on a sandwich, "That's OK, Gene. I talked to Joe and had him put spring water in the tractor radiator. I told him spring water wouldn't freeze."

Gene thought about it a moment, jumped up, spilled his coffee, left his unfinished lunch, and hurried to Joe's place to retrieve his tractor.

Bob's steady job at the Experimental Farm kept us going financially. By 1957, the Farmer's Home Administration granted us a $20,000 loan to buy cows, build a milking parlor, clear 100 acres, put a basement under our house, and add a porch.

I said, "Bob, do you realize operating a dairy is a seven-day-a-week, two-times-a-day job?"

Bob looked up and replied, "I'm not going anywhere anyway."

IMC Anderson, the head of the FHA, brought the check to our home, and set it on the table. When I saw the check and the payment schedule, with different amounts of money for each FHA qualification expected on a dairy, I thought 1994 was a long ways off, but we weren't going anywhere anyway.

Bob told me later he really did have second thoughts and wondered what he was getting into.

The first step in clearing land, was to hire a bulldozer and operator. The dozer skimmed off the trees, pushed them into stump rows and inevitably left roots, branches, and broken tree stumps in the field, as if a cyclone had touched down.

The next step was when the work really started. We had to loosen, pick up, and throw leftover tree limbs, roots, and stumps, into the stump row. Rocks of various sizes were uncovered as the dozer did it's job. Rocks could cause extensive damage to farm machinery, so our whole family spent much of the summer clearing fields of rocks. It took a special plow, called

a breaking plow, pulled by a bulldozer, to break up the soil the first time. An ordinary farm plow was not strong enough to cut through roots and move rocks. After breaking the land, we could till and plant our crops.

After clearing and yanking up roots, we burned the stump rows. Some spring and summer days, the valley air was hazy-blue with wood smoke.

Later, a bulldozer scattered the burned stump rows and remaining debris was restacked to be burned again. This left a large field with no stump row. Cleaning up; stump rows could take many years.

It wasn't unusual for a stump-row fire to smolder for months. Large piles of wood and dirt mixed in with debris could smolder even on cold, winter days. You could see wisps of smoke rising from stump rows all winter. Occasionally, we heard stories of children playing around stump rows, falling into concealed holes, and being severely burned.

We hired a Wasilla contractor, who owned a small bulldozer, to excavate the basement for our house. While there, we had him dig a cesspool hole in the back yard. We warned the kids to stay away from the hole. The sides could collapse and bury them. Bob, on his way into the house for lunch one day, heard a timid soft voice.

"Roger, Roger. Come and get me, Roger."

Bob scouted around and found Barbara at the bottom of the cesspool hole. She couldn't get out without help and was calling Roger, her big brother, in her time of need. She was a child who never panicked or got excited.

Bob slid down into the hole, helped her out, and crawled out himself. Both came to lunch as if nothing had happened. As long as no one was hurt, I didn't get excited. Barbara needed no more warnings to convince her to stay away from the hole.

After we built the basement, we had a professional house-mover from Anchorage move the house onto the walls. His five-year-old son, chewing snuff and spitting tobacco juice like a man, accompanied him. When the mover was ready to move the house, he asked me to put a full glass of water on the kitchen table. I stood by the table as he moved the house inch by inch. He didn't spill a drop of water.

Bob took advantage of the Anchorage Housing Authority remodeling project and purchased a used coal and wood combination furnace for $100.

Occasionally, Bob took Roger and Barbara with him to buy coal from the Jonesville mine, near Sutton, about a 35-mile trip, one way. He used the old 1948 1 and 1/2-ton Studebaker farm truck with broken windows, floor boards that let in daylight, and no heater. Bob dressed extra warm, and the kids wrapped up in blankets and toughed it out on these coal-hauling junkets. They preferred the chilly outing to staying home doing chores.

On a cold, winter evening, we were enjoying a quiet time in the living room. One of the kids heard a moose tromping in the snow, close to the house.

Bob said to us, as he tiptoed to the door, "Watch this."

When the moose got close to the door, Bob flung it open and yelled, "Boo!"

The startled moose struck out with his front feet. Bob jumped back in the house, "I almost shook hands with that moose!" We all laughed and watched the moose lumber away into the woods.

Our family cow, Petunia, produced more milk than we could consume each day. We sold a gallon for a dollar to Elaine Harris, our nearest neighbor. We agreed that when the bill amounted to $40, she would pay me. One of her kids walked to our place to pick up the milk. One day, Elaine came over and paid the bill. I immediately made out an order to Sears and Roebuck for linoleum for the kitchen and living room floors, and rushed in to Wasilla and mailed the order. I knew, in homestead life, most money went to fix this and that in the fields or barns. Improvements in the home were last on the priority list.

When Bob came in for dinner that day, he announced he needed a new part for his tractor. I said, "Don't you have any money?"

"No!" he quipped back. "I thought you did. I saw Elaine here this morning and thought she paid you for the milk she's been getting."

I snapped back, "Aha, I fixed you. As soon as she paid me I went to Wasilla and bought a money order for new linoleum. I figured this would happen. Case closed!"

Don Church cleared the 100 acres, required by FHA, in the spring of 1957. He also broke ground and got it ready for planting, then Bob had to disc, harrow, and seed. He planted oats and peas to be used as silage, and barley for feed grain.

Our cows, a motley-looking herd of Jerseys, were a sad sight when they arrived at our farm in the driving rain aboard a cattle truck from Minnesota. Bob and the two drivers unloaded the cows from the truck into the pen. We stood in the rain and looked them over. We were stuck with eight Jersey cows that didn't look too promising. At the end of two years, most of them had been disposed of, because they were such poor producers. We gradually built our herd of 30 cows with Jersey, Holstein, Guernsey, and Brown Swiss.

Through the years, the cow barn was a place of tranquil discussions between father and son, occasionally a place of activity, and sometimes one of discipline for an ornery critter unwilling to be broken to a stanchion or when a kicker was reprimanded with a doubled-up fist.

When the birth of a calf was eminent, we herded the prospective mother into a small maternity shed piled deep with extra clean straw. Here the pregnant cow could give birth in quiet, peaceful surroundings. After the birth, she took her long, rough tongue and massaged her baby and encouraged it to stand. This process created a bond between mother and baby. This ritual also stimulated the baby to seek its first important meal, consisting of colostrum milk filled with: proteins, minerals, antibodies, and natural vitamins. When a birth was about to take place, and it wasn't in the middle of the night, the kids and I rushed to the maternity shed to watch. The kids, with wide, excited eyes, were awed by the process.

The Barnes family, living close by, heard our story of birthing calves. Mrs. Barnes asked me to notify her when the next calf was to be born. She wanted her children to observe the event. I remember six kids hanging over a fence watching this miracle.

Barbara, about eight years old, said to me, as I explained that humans and animals gave birth in a similar way, "Oh, Yuck! I'm never going to have a baby."

Births weren't always easy. Complications could arise, and it was important that the prospective mother had assistance. A calf's head or leg might need to be turned in the right direction before a successful birth. At times a veterinarian would be needed. Sometimes, after listening to a cow bellow in agony for hours, she would give birth to a still-born calf. This was a sad occasion. Our family had to listen to the new mother cry for her baby until she finally accepted the inevitable.

During winter months, we confined the cows to the feeding lot next to the barn. In spring and summer, the kids escorted them across the road to green pasture. There, the kids explored and communed with nature while keeping track of the cows. They picked wild flowers, gathered and played with frogs, and fought mosquitoes. It didn't take long for the herd to know their boundaries. The kids were delighted when, after many years, we built fences and they were no longer required to tag after the cows. To this day, the kids brag about herding cows where Snowshoe Grade School stands.

Cows are placid animals, not inclined to hurry. Their slow pace sometimes aggravated the kids. When it was time to bring the herd back to the barn, the kids resorted to tail-twisting, colorful language or prodding with sticks.

As soon as green grass was abundant, Roger drove the tractor and silage chopper to the fields. Bob drove the farm truck, and they harvested green feed and brought it back to the lot for the cows. This process ended the herding chores.

Bovine population on our property was very important. We butchered unproductive milk cows for our use or sold them to the slaughter house. Each had their own distinct trait. Generally, they were tame, but there was always the occasional wild one. Each cow had their unique personality and their own descriptive name.

Melanie - a Jersey secured from another dairyman because she didn't fit in his herd, was a wonderful family cow for us.

Petunia - a Holstein, raised by our family, started our herd.

Bonnie - a Brown Swiss, grand champion at the Alaska State Fair.

Flossie - a big, brassy, bossy Holstein.

Tess - a Holstein born with six teats.

Breezy - a Jersey fence jumper, who met her demise in our front yard after jumping the fence for the last time.

Snowball - a pure white Holstein.

Bones - a Jersey, our skinniest cow, but an excellent producer.

Windy - a Jersey, one of our best.

Gershy - a Holstein that suckled the other cows.

Peanuts - a Holstein steer we raised for beef.

Lollypop - a Brown Swiss, good producer. Blind in one eye and couldn't see an electric fence and was shocked many times.

Stormy and Sunny - our best Jersey producers.

Oleo and Margarine - Holstein twins.

Pete and Repeat - Jersey twins.

Each year, we named the new-born calves more or less along the same lines, like snacks, people, flowers, weather, or after the looks of the animal. It was fun to come up with appropriate names. It was also advantageous, because we could remember what year they were born.

Bob quit his job at the Experimental Farm and devoted all his time to dairying in 1957. The kids and I would have milked the cows if he'd continued to work at the Experimental Farm, but working for himself had been a life-long dream. Whatever money the dairy made was invested back into the project.

We made small, monthly payments on a 21-foot freezer. I continued to keep grocery bills low by making jelly, baking bread, picking berries, canning pickles, and freezing vegetables. We had all the meat, eggs, milk, and cream we could use.

We hired a builder to construct a concrete block milking parlor, using the herringbone system originating in New Zealand. It held the cows being milked at a slant, thus we needed no stanchions and the cows kept each other in line. We fed them grain while they were being milked with an automatic milking machine.

Bob's herringbone system was the first in Alaska, and one of the first in the United States. He built a large loafing barn near the milking parlor. Here, we stored hay and fed the cows. We built the building from used telephone poles and covered it with galvanized tin.

While in the dairy business, Bob never had a garage or a machine shed, a real detriment to the operation of our dairy.

One night, Bob and I were at a political meeting at the Wasilla School. During a question-and-answer period, a resident asked the speaker about Social Security benefits.

The speaker answered, "I can't give you an answer on that. Every time it comes up in the Senate, it's utter confusion."

I immediately poked Bob in the ribs and said, "That's the name of our dairy, Udder Confusion!"

The name immediately stuck, and soon appeared on a sign at the beginning of our driveway and on our car. The sign was on a half-sheet of plywood painted yellow. The black, crossed-eyed cow on the sign had a wisp of hay hanging from her mouth. Her tail formed the U in the title

Udder Confusion. The pink udder of the cow formed the letters of Udder Confusion.

We acquired a brown and white, short-legged, Shetland pony named Friday. A local farm family in Palmer coerced Bob into taking care of Friday. He thought the pony would be a good pet for the kids. Friday didn't impress the kids much, and soon they were complaining about him.

"Here you have a pony to ride and you're not riding him. Why?" I asked.

"We don't, because he won't let us. When Friday gets tired of us on his back, he lays down or scrapes us off against a tree, building or the Volkswagon. You know, he dumps us into mud puddles every time he gets a chance!"

Whenever Bob turned the cows into pasture, Friday went too. When it was time to bring the cows back to the barn, Bob walked to the pasture and called, "Come boss. Come boss." When Friday heard Bob, he assumed the responsibility of rounding up the cows and driving them to the corral gate. As the cows headed to the gate, Friday went ahead of them, stood at the corral gate, and bit each one on the rump as they came through. The cows knew Friday would nip, so they bunched up and hurried through the gate. To make matters worse, Friday continued to harass and provoke the cows feeding alongside the silo. We noticed milk production began dropping. Bob blamed Friday's skirmishes. Milking cows was more important to the family than a pony who thought he was a rancher. Finally, without tears, we called the owners to come and get him.

A bunker silo is made on top of the ground. Bob made his with two rows of railroad ties stacked on their sides. The silo was 12 feet across at the bottom, and tapered to 16 feet at the top. Pillars braced the ties every five feet. The silo was 50-feet long.

Roger and Bob picked up discarded railroad ties along the railroad tracks. This was hard work, but all it cost was muscle power and a truck to bring them home.

Bob made a sling to lay in the bed of the truck and filled it with silage at harvest time. To fill the silo, Bob drove the truck into the silo and attached another vehicle to the sling, containing the silage. He'd drive the truck forward from under the filled sling. The more silage put into the silo, the higher up into the silo we had to drive the truck.

One day, Bob put a load of silage into the silo. When he drove too close to the right side, he got the right wheels stuck between the silage and the side of the silo. Bob was working by himself and couldn't get the truck out. He came to the house and asked me to steer the truck while he pulled it out with a borrowed truck. When I saw the situation, I refused to drive. I was afraid the truck would tip over. Bob got angry and I went back to the house. He hooked onto the truck in the silo, gave a hard, angry tug, and a section of the right wall gave way. He spent the rest of the day, and half of the next, repairing the silo. In the fall, when the silo was full, my spirits soared. No longer would Bob call me from my own projects for help.

"Please pass the potatoes." Bob looked out the window. "Carpenter's calves are in the silo again. Come on, kids, help me put them back where they belong."

Four newly-purchased calves belonging to Carpenter, an absentee neighbor, had ruined another lunch, and everyone but me scurried after Bob as he threw rocks at the renegades. Carpenter, who was nearly ready for retirement, lived and worked in Anchorage, but spent weekends and vacations at his ranch. For him, ranching consisted of puttering around, petting his calves, and nailing up a board or two here and there.

High hopes of retiring to his ranch were going to end abruptly if he didn't keep his herd from constantly dining out of our bunker silo. We were tired of feeding his animals to further his ambition of raising stock to sell as bred heifers to local dairymen.

Carpenter hired neighborhood kids to daily feed and water the livestock in his absence. At first, each kid thought the job was easy pickings for $2 a day. After packing water, carrying hay, shoveling manure, and doing other chores connected with calf raising, they soon changed their minds and none stayed long. Wayne, the last man hired, lasted the longest.

Calves require food, water, and friends. When left alone, Carpenter's steers and heifers became lonesome and hungry. Forcing their way through the fence, they wandered down the road looking for companionship and something to eat.

Bob was irritated by the regular visits of the four calves. They upset our whole family. Nothing is more discouraging than coming home from town, or looking out the window, and seeing four young calves devouring the peas and oats in the bunker silo. It was even worse to see them grazing on the tops of our garden vegetables.

The plague lasted over a year. Tempers at our place flared as Carpenter's calves became a constant nuisance.

Our visits to Carpenter in Anchorage failed to convince him to keep his stock corralled. He embarrassed us and arrogantly refused to help in anyway with solutions.

Carpenter would shout, "There's no herd laws in Alaska, and there's nothing you can do about it." After pleading and threatening, our patience and nerves wore thin—very thin!

In the spring of Carpenter's last year of ranching, he purchased a young Holstein bull. He figured his retirement and dream of raising dairy stock would be bolstered by purchasing this bull.

Calf visits became more frequent and troublesome by the addition of this young, virile gentleman of the herd. One day, the calves, with their bull escort, made a visit. As he neared our place the bull spotted our herd of cows. Like most bulls in spring, and in the presence of heifers, he started showing his masculinity and pawed the ground. Roaring, snorting, and bellowing, he asserted that he was boss around "these here parts!"

By the time the school bus brought the kids home, the bull was at the height of his strutting and rutting performance. Bob mothered the kids to the house and then tried to persuade the bull to leave the premises. None of his urging or threats worked. The bull planted himself firmly between the house and the barn and defied Bob to come near. The closer Bob got, the nastier the bull became. He'd lower his head, snort warnings and, with his front feet, throw dirt in all directions.

Bob gave up and called the State Troopers. Distance separates places in Alaska and, even at emergency speed, a Trooper took over 20 minutes to get to our farm. Meanwhile, the standoff between Bob and the bull continued.

The brave Trooper drove into the yard, swiftly surveyed the scene, and refused to leave his car. That bull was pretty spectacular!

"That's definitely a vicious animal," the Trooper exclaimed to Bob through a partly open window. Radioing his superior, and making sure headquarters could hear the ranting bull over the microphone, the Trooper asked for advice.

"Do what you have to do to get the animal out of there, but don't shoot unless the bull is actually attacking a person. Do the best you can."

"How can we get the bull out of here?" the trooper asked Bob.

"I know how I'll get him out of here," Bob hinted as he ran to the diesel tractor, his newest piece of equipment, and his pride and joy.

Safely gaining the tractor, Bob started the motor, raised the front-end loader attachment halfway, and charged the bull. The bull protected his territory, pawed the ground, snorted some more, and held firm. Bob caught the love-struck bull just above the knees and shoved him again and again, finally out of the yard, across the fields, and back to Carpenter's barn.

Still in his patrol car, and laughing so hard he could hardly drive, the Trooper followed.

That March, the calves were two years old and in fine shape. By this time we were thoroughly disgusted with them and their owner. There didn't seem to be a way we could keep the marauders out. Silage and hay bales were disappearing rapidly. Green grazing grasses for our herd would not be available until the first part of June. The plundering intensified. Vile language and defamation of Carpenter's character was the main dinner table conversation. The calves were fed—but we were fed up!

Days later, while the kids were in school, at the height of our anger and frustration, the four calves, minus the bull, sauntered into our yard and headed for the silo. We'd talked and joked about how we could balance the ledger for feeding Carpenter's cattle for nearly two years, but always before today it was only idle threats. When we saw the four fat freezer-potentials heading for their stolen dinner, we acted.

Together, we separated the herd by driving the biggest and fattest one into our barn, then sent the other three scattering for home. Bob went into the barn and settled the feed bill with Carpenter. He was just finishing the harvesting when Wayne, the hired man, drove into our yard looking for the lost calf. He headed straight to the barn. Bob heard him coming and hurriedly met him at the door, diverting his attention by walking with him to the house for a cup of coffee. They talked about recent reports of a grizzly bear in the area. Along with that scare, Bob added the fact that bears were awake early because of an earthquake.

The caretaker believed him and decided to walk through the bogs and woods to see if he could find any bear tracks. He spent most of the next four or five days looking for the missing calf. When he wasn't looking for the lost calf, he kept the remainder of the herd home. He never found the calf, but he did find plenty of bear tracks.

He reported to Carpenter that he hadn't found the lost calf and there were bear tracks in the surrounding area. It was likely the bear had killed the calf.

This was discouraging news for Carpenter. He became disenchanted with his ranching dream and within a few months sold the remaining livestock.

"Please pass the potatoes—and the tender beef roast.

Some of our favorite times were picking berries from the middle of summer until fall. Our kids didn't always think it was fun, but it kept them busy and also provided a source of fruit for winter.

In 1918, a forest fire swept the Wasilla area. In the open burned areas, lowbush cranberries grew profusely. A favorite dessert was cooked, sweetened cranberries folded into fresh-whipped cream from our dairy.

In the damp, boggy areas of the woods, we found red and black currants, which we used for jelly. Each year, I made at least 50 pints of jams and jellies, which served our yearly needs. On Sundays, the kids took turns picking out their favorite jam or jelly. It had to last all week.

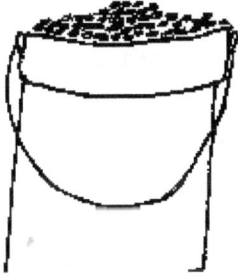

We found highbush cranberries in the dryer areas of the woods. They made a jelly closely resembling apple butter. We always knew when the highbush cranberries were ripe and ready to pick—the woods smelled like dirty feet!

We found red raspberries in old stump rows. The kids and I crawled over old, rotten logs and tangled undergrowth to get to them. At times, we had to compete with the yellow jackets for berries. We fastened gallon buckets to our belts so both hands would be free to pick berries. Raspberries not made into jam, were served with sugar and cream.

Our family's favorite berry was the blueberry. Once a year, we took a day off to pick this delicious berry. By ourselves, or with friends, we'd pack a picnic lunch, pile into pickups, and drive 17 miles to the mountains, where the best-producing blueberry patches thrived.

Most years, we picked six gallons of blueberries on each excursion. Bob and Roger used a special berry-picking comb. I didn't particularly like the comb. It scooped up leaves and trash, as well as the berries, making more work for myself when I cleaned them.

We arrived home fatigued from climbing around on the mountains, crossing streams, and crawling through the alders. Sometimes, we got thoroughly soaked by a warm summer rain. We never saw a bear while picking berries. I guess we were too noisy.

Blueberry-picking trips were always relived during the winter, as we sat around the table eating tasty pie, muffins, or syrup poured over pancakes or waffles.

When Barbara and Linda were young, they were more of a liability than an asset in the berry patches. They complained—they were tired, there were too many mosquitoes, or they couldn't find any berries. They spilled the few they had. Barbara tried many times to fill her bucket 3/4 full of leaves, filled the top 1/4 with berries and considered that fair play. One year when she was older, she refused to pick a single blueberry. She sat on a log and complained. That winter, when I served blueberry pie, her allotment was a slice so small it amounted to only a taste. She must of learned her lesson because the next year she picked her share. My philosophy was "No workee—no eatee."

Bob and Roger picked hour after hour. If the picking was good, I enjoyed it, if not I tolerated it. In due time Linda became quite proficient at picking berries. Barbara couldn't wait to pick berries after she grew up and returned home for visits.

Our favorite and most convenient cranberry patch was located four miles from home. I could pick a gallon of berries in an hour, but as the years went by it took longer and longer to fill my bucket. I heard that a cranberry patch's life span is seven years. When the brush grows up in and around the patch, the berries diminish. We were always on the lookout for a new patch.

Harold and Elaine Harris were like most homesteading families; free thinkers, diverse in their doings, friendly and helpful. They wanted 12 children, had six and changed their mind after three. Harold was not religious, but believed in the laying-on of hands when it came to disciplining his children.

Harold was a giant of a man, a workaholic with a head full of homesteading dreams. He had an appetite to match his stature and liked his pies round. Elaine, was a two -year college graduate, a city girl willing to learn even though ignorant of country living. She once painted the basement concrete floor battleship gray and then immediately put newspaper down.

"Why did you put newspaper down on the wet paint?" I asked.

She replied with pride, "So the children won't leave their muddy foot prints on my nice, new floor."

We could read the newsprint for months.

When Harold worked off the farm, Elaine would send him on his way, with a sack full of sandwiches and a quart of milk. He balanced his pie in one upturned hand.

Anything he owned, you were welcome to borrow. It worked the other way as well. If there was anything Harold needed, he borrowed it, sometimes without asking.

One winter, he borrowed a logging chain from Bob. He promised to bring it back promptly. Time went by and he hadn't kept his promise. Bob asked Harold when he was going to return it. It was winter, and I'm sure he had many uses for it around his farm. One day, Harold drove his tractor from his place, past our place, to another neighbor's. As he neared our driveway, he threw the chain off to one side of the road.

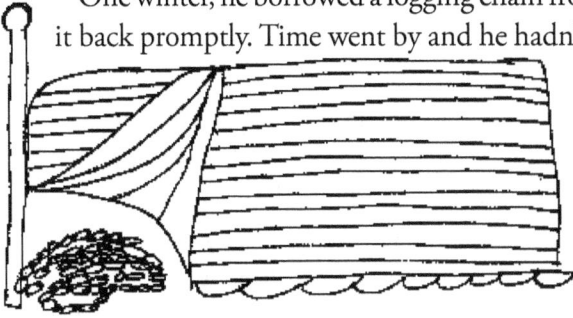

We were in town, so we knew nothing of the return. Later, Bob again asked for his chain. Harold told him he'd returned it a couple of weeks earlier. In the meantime it had snowed several times and the chain was buried in a snowdrift. We didn't receive the chain back until spring. Harold's heart was in the right place but, sometimes we wondered where he kept his brain.

That winter, Bob was cutting wood for our own stove and decided to invest in a new logging chain. His borrowed chain was too short, lightweight, and didn't have what he thought were proper hooks.

In order to keep Harold from borrowing his new chain, Bob decided to keep it under our bed, secure from this neighbor who snooped through our buildings. Whenever Bob came into the house for his logging chain, I teased him. "I'm sure glad no one saw you dragging a logging chain from underneath our bed!" Bob just grinned and went on about his work.

Harold's neighbors up and down the road for miles were weary of his hogs roaming the countryside, getting into gardens and fields, and generally making a nuisance of themselves. Harold deliberately turned his hogs out at night to forage for themselves. Early in the mornings, we heard him calling them, "Su-u-e-e-e, Su-u-e-e-e!" to entice them home with a promise of grain for breakfast. They pestered the Erickson brothers to distraction by rooting out and eating their commercial potato crop. Once, Harold went to the Erickson homestead looking for his wayward trespassers and found the Erickson brothers butchering one of his hogs.

Waldo handed Harold a knife and said "Get busy!" He did. Waldo later gave Harold a roast from his own hog.

During one of our early summers on the homestead, Harold's 300 pound sow came visiting daily. The sow was a real nuisance. It damaged my garden, scared the kids, and upset the dogs and cows. Harold was working away from home, so we complained to Elaine. She was either busy with small children, or about to deliver another, and couldn't do much about the situation. We knew this and sympathized with her, but something had to be done.

After one of our complaints, Elaine suggested Bob butcher the sow and we take half in payment for damage and nuisance. Bob jumped at the offer. A day later, he dressed out the sow, processed it into roasts, chops, and sausage, and wrapped and delivered her portion. Now, we were both rid of the problem and both happy with the supply of meat. I rendered seven gallons of lard from our half of the animal. There is nothing finer than pie crust made with pure lard.

For months, until all the pork was consumed, our table was set for meals with an extra dish placed at the center of the table to collect buckshot found in the cooked meat. Bob never used buckshot on the farm, so this sow must have made herself a nuisance at many other farms before she bothered us.

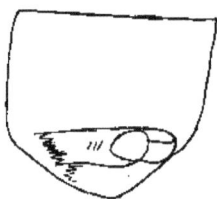

One day, Bob was cutting a small board on the saw for one of the kid's projects. He was working from the back side of the saw blade, guiding a board with a knot in it. Knots are harder to saw than the rest of the board. When the blade worked through the knot, it quickly ripped through the wood—and Bob's fingers. He automatically jerked his hands toward himself and cut off the tips of three fingers. He picked up the fingers and put them in his shirt pocket. He managed to climb onto the tractor and drive to the Combs' farm to see if he could get someone to take him to the doctor in Palmer.

Our farm truck was broken down and I had the car and was picking strawberries at a friend's, who lived near Palmer. There was no car at the Combs' house either. Mary Combs told her son, Billy, to get on the tractor and get Harold Harris so he could take Bob to Palmer. That was another mile to go back past our farm again and another half-mile to the Harris'. Harold finally came to the Combs' farm in his old Packard car. Bob said he would've rather walked because Harold drove 90-miles-an-hour on 13 miles of crooked, graveled roads to Palmer Hospital. A nurse's aid got information from Bob about my whereabouts and drove out to the strawberry patch to inform me of the accident.

Bob lay on the gurney in the emergency room smoking a cigarette. Dr. Colberg came in and shouted, "Who said you could smoke in here. Now, I'll have to put your fingers and fingertips in a stronger sterilizing solution."

When the doctor started sewing the fingertips back on, he noticed there was only two. Harold then got back in his car and madly drove back to get the other finger.

After checking that Bob was all right, I drove home. The children had been left alone too long. Blood was all over the meat saw tray, on the walls, and had dripped on the floor and out the door. The fingertip retrieved by Harold had been laying on the tray of the saw was the only one that grew back. In a month's time, it was obvious the two black tips would never grow back. Bob always teased it was because the doctor sterilized the other two fingers too much.

Ours was a family business. Bob and Roger did the muscle work. Roger could drive the tractor at 10 years of age, and thought he was hot stuff until one day he was helping Bob hook up a trailer.

"Back it up a little, Roger."

Roger did, and stalled the tractor on Bob's foot. Roger was flustered and couldn't start the tractor again.

"You're on my foot!" shouted Bob. He reached past Roger, threw the tractor into gear, grabbed the tractor tire-tread and rolled it off his foot. Rubbing his foot, thankful for soft soil, and to ease the boy's mind, Bob said, "It's OK. You're still my right-hand man."

The girls helped make silage and haul bales of hay, herd cows, and do anything else they could at their young age. I was the truck driver and "gopher"—go for this and go for that—plus being chief cook and bottle washer.

Roger took scraps of lumber and built a tree house high in the branches of a nearby cottonwood tree. The girls spent many hours in their playhouse. Whenever I needed them, I knew where they'd be.

Free help on the farm is every farmer's dream, especially if that help is from his wife. Two of the duties expected of me was truck and tractor driver. These jobs had to be done, even if I was in the middle of a big project of my own, such as canning green beans or freezing broccoli. I was willing to help where I could, but I refused to milk cows.

I told Bob, "There are two men on this place. They can milk the cows."

I also refused to burn shecan wood—she can chop the wood, she can bring it in, and she can take out the ashes.

One beautiful, fall day, Bob drove the tractor, while I was conscripted to ride the borrowed binder, a machine that bundles the ripe grain and throws it on the ground. At first, things went along smoothly. Then, as usual, the binder gears and cogs plugged up and caused the operation to cease. After much cussing at the machinery, Bob finally lashed out at me as if I'd caused the mess. I listened for a while, then I got upset.

I got off the binder seat and shouted at him, " You sure treat your free help rotten. If I'd been working for wages, I would have quit long ago." I stomped to the house, kicking clods of dirt all the way.

Hours later, when the problem was fixed, he sheepishly walked back to the house.

"Did you finally get it fixed?" I chided. Without an answer or another word, I followed him to the field and we proceeded with our task. Some men can't apologize, but do so by being nice, cooperative, or extra cheerful for a few hours. Bob was this way.

At times, jobs on the farm were almost impossible without extra help. We had no money for hiring help, so during harvesttime couples from neighboring farms got together and worked, first at one place, then another. The two women would drive trucks, one man the tractor and silage chopper. The other man leveled out the silage, filled in low spots, and knocked off the high spots in between loads. The women stayed with the trucks until just before the noon meal. The two men finished unloading the trucks at the silo, while we put a meal on the table, usually of roast, potatoes, gravy, vegetables, and dessert of pie or cake.

Out in the fields, farmer-husbands had little or no patience with their wives. But, with neighbor's wives they were gentle and patient. We wives threatened to go to work for each others husbands. Maybe we would get some respect if we "wife-swapped" during harvest time.

We had running water, all right. First we ran in with it, and then ran out with it. When the water cans were empty, Bob went for more and, once he got there, the neighbors were great people to visit. He wouldn't come back for hours. I ranted and raved, while he was enjoying himself.

Bob accused me at times, "What did you do with all that water?"

I snapped back with anger in my voice, "I dump it on the ground just to make you get more."

"I believe it!" he shouted, and stomped out the door.

One of the requirements of an FHA loan was to drill a well. Herb Boucher witched the well depth and location. He said it would be 120 feet, and it was, exactly. The water rose to within 32 feet of the surface. It produced in excess of 1,200 gallons per hour. The water was 34° in the summer and 36° in the winter. It seemed it should be the other way, warmer in summer and colder in winter, but it wasn't. Bob built a small concrete building over the well to protect it from the elements and piped the water to the house. It was the first running water into the house in the eight years we lived in Alaska.

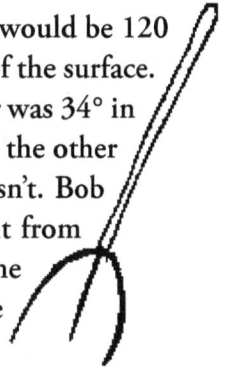

We heated water with furnace coils. If the furnace was shut down or wasn't running, there wasn't much hot water. Even then, hot water seemed like a luxury, compared to heating it on the stove for bathing and laundry. I always maintained that if anyone on a homestead ever got a divorce, it was over water or wood.

We acquired a newborn bull calf during this time. When it grew bigger, Bob put a ring in the calf's nose for a lead. He snapped a chain about eight-inches long into his nose ring. One day, he accidentally touched the chain on the electric corral fence. It jolted the bull so bad, it actually made tears come to his eyes.

Eventually, Bob loaned him to a neighbor for breeding purposes. Bob later found out the farmer had jabbed the bull in the ribs with a pitchfork, eventually causing the bull's death. The veterinarian and Dr. Brundage, from the Experimental Station, performed an autopsy on him and found adhesions. His stomach had grown to his side. The vet said that in this case, it was caused by being punctured by a sharp instrument. It had to be the neighbor who was guilty of this vile act, because Bob was never mean to his cattle.

If school was not in session, Roger drove the tractor when we were making silage, Bob drove the tractor. When the kids were in school, it was my turn.

I remember one incident during harvest, as we were going round and round the field filling the truck with silage, the truck stopped abruptly. Bob was driving the tractor and was carefully watching where he was going. Naturally, it was some time before he noticed that I wasn't alongside of him with the truck, and the silage was spewing onto the ground. He came back to the truck and demanded to know why I couldn't keep up with him. I told him I thought the truck had run out of gas. I'd driven enough cars, trucks, and tractors to know how motors act when they run out of gas. He lifted the hood of the truck to look for the trouble. I could see him beginning to seethe because he couldn't find what was wrong. After 15 minutes, I got bullheaded and gave him a piece of my mind. I gave him my usual tirade of how he treated his free help.

It was nearing milking time, and he'd already spent more than an hour exploring the trouble. He gave up, came to the house and said, "Guess I'll have to check it out again tomorrow morning. I sure can't find out what's wrong tonight."

The following morning, after milking and chores were done, he marched out to the truck again, determined to find the root of the trouble. In about 15 minutes, he came back to the gas barrels, looking pretty meek and humble.

I said, "Was it out of gas?"

No answer. He was in no mood to listen to any comments from me. We silently walked to the truck. I watched him pour gas into the tank, and we worked the rest of the day with no trouble.

In 1961, we bought a used Volkswagon bus. This bus was originally built as an ambulance, but it wasn't built to the buyer's specifications. The new owner put it up for sale after using it for two years. It was empty in the back, except for the drawers and cupboards under the beds around the edge. Bob thought it was perfect for hauling feed, tools, and farm supplies, but it was never designed to be a farmer's truck and we overworked it.

Bob never hated a car so much. He put three rebuilt motors in it, the heater never worked, it drank oil by the quart, and it was hard to start. It always plagued us with mechanical problems.

Each time something went wrong, Bob would proclaim, long and loud, "It's no wonder I can't get along with that Volkswagon. I have a German wife, a German car, but can't even cuss in German."

I had a few scary experiences with the bus myself. One evening, coming home from work, I slid sideways into a deep ditch, spun a few crooked circles, drove up on the icy road, and arrived home, acting as if nothing had happened.

Another time, I was coming home from a friend's

who had started a permanent in my hair. Near our home I slowed down to turn into our driveway. The wind picked up the bus and slammed it over onto the driver's side. I was uninjured and crawled out with a white bath towel around my head. I had planned to finish my permanent at home.

When the kids found out I was safe, they started laughing. They said I looked like a chipmunk crawling out of a hole. We were amazed I wasn't hurt. Two large, round tractor weights were behind the driver's seat, which could've come forward and killed me. I was shaking with fear. As the kids helped me to the house, I calmed down and we had a good laugh together.

While we waited for the wind to stop roaring, Bob called the insurance company. The next day, they sent a tow truck to haul the VW into Wasilla for repairs. While the repairs were being done, I had to find a ride to work. (When Linda entered second grade, I began working in an office in Palmer to help make ends meet.) Florence Dunlap, who lived in Palmer, was a good friend and invited me to stay with her during that week, and I walked to work close by. The insurance company paid the bill, including the tow charge, but they charged us $200 extra for three years until they recouped the $600.

Our vendetta with the VW came to a climax in 1963, when we traded the worn-out bus for a new Ford Falcon. I was happy to make the payments for reliable transportation. Although small, the Falcon was a good car.

Money conditions on the farm got a lot slimmer. We thought the milk check would be enough to keep us, but we didn't get as much as we thought we would for milk. We had a butterfat test of 6%, but the Co-op paid us for the maximum allowed of 4.5%, which put us out of a considerable amount of money. We managed, but it was tough. Everyone in the family had to work. Barbara fed calves and Roger worked in the fields with Bob, chopping silage, mowing hay, and twice-a-day, milking cows. Linda helped out where she was able.

We may not have made any money on the dairy, but the kids learned about good honest work.

By 1964, things were going from bad to worse on the dairy. We weren't making enough money to support the cows. Milk was worth 12 cents a pound when we started the dairy. It dropped to eight cents a pound and was still costing eight 1/2 cents a pound to produce.

Prices had dropped because milk from Washington State was being shipped into Alaska cheaper than we could produce it and distribute it within the state. We were in need of more machinery and more cows in order to make ends meet. Roger was planning on attending college the following year and would no longer be there to help. We decided to sell our herd in the summer of 1964.

A local dairyman purchased the cows, and all money received, we turned over to the FHA for back debts. We sold all the farm machinery and milking equipment to help toward financial freedom.

When the cows were loaded into a huge cattle truck, we had mixed emotions—sadness and relief. The morning after the cows left the farm, Bob arose as usual, walked the floor and said to me, "I don't have anything to do now."

After we sold the dairy herd, there was a more relaxed, carefree atmosphere around the farm. No more dawn-to-dark laboring. We had more time to talk and think of the future and discuss the past. Udder Confusion was out of business, but we continued to live on the farm, and I still had my job in Palmer. Bob worked for a few weeks at odd jobs on the farm he couldn't seem to get to before, and thought about going back to work for a regular paycheck.

In the spring of 1965, Bob went to work for Barney Hollembeck and Rick Loyer, partners of Knik Supply. At first, he was unloading grains and feeds from railroad cars and assembling farm machinery. After he was there for three days, Rick asked him to tend the feed store while he was gone for a few hours. Rick, with money from the cash drawer in hand, left an IOU and would be gone all day.

Bob ended up in charge of the store, full time. He had to make many decisions, as well as get balled out by irate customers. He told one ornery customer, "You want my supplies and I want your money. So why can't we both use good manners and accomplish what we set out to do."

Bob learned about ordering feeds, machinery, and parts. He thought anyone working in a store or office should never get tired as no physical effort was expended. He learned different, and came home worn out and told of people he met; everyone from spoiled pet lovers to hard working farmers.

It was while working for Knik Supply, Bob made out a Civil Service application for a meat cutter job on Elmendorf Air Force Base. He didn't hear anything about it until November 1965. He started work on the base as a journeyman meat cutter for $3.38 an hour. It was hard work, but steady.

We now had time to take a weekend or a month-long trip every year, if we so desired. The kids were in high school and we were now able to take a more active part in their activities.

In 1967, we sold the homestead to a family who were just as anxious to be ranchers as we once were. The transition from dairying to non-dairying was gradual and pleasant. From then on it wasn't, "Please pass the milk". It was, "Please pass the canned cow."

Udder Confusion
Photo Album

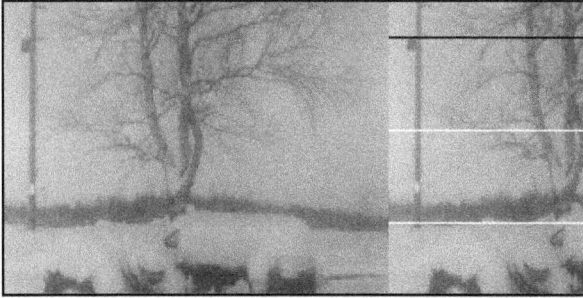

We traded our small car for a new 3/4-ton Studebaker pickup. The racks stored tools, boxes, trunks, canned goods, spare tires, extra clothing, small appliances, baby furniture, and even an old refrigerator we thought we couldn't get along without in Alaska. On April Fool's Day, 1950, a clear and windy spring day, amid sentimental good-byes and good luck wishes from relatives and friends, we left Yakima and headed for Alaska.

During the 1930s, 180 farmers from the Midwest colonized in the Matanuska Valley under the Alaska Rural Rehabilitation Corporation. This federal program helped families suffering from the depression. There were many houses and barns built after the same pattern.

Wasilla was a small town consisting of a school, post office, roadhouse, service station, and a dozen or so houses. Wasilla served an area of approximately 500 people.

"I have a small, two-room cabin," Annie interjected. "I could rent it to you for $25 a month. It has no electricity. You'll have to bail water. Besides, I need a family to buy my fresh eggs and milk."

At the end of May, it was time to start planting a garden. I sought advice about which vegetables would grow and how much fertilizer to apply. As a novice at gardening, I planted peas, onions, carrots, lettuce, cabbage, potatoes, radishes, Swiss chard, and green beans. The long hours of summer sunlight and plenty of rain caused the vegetables, including a lot of weeds, to grow into giants.

After fishing season came and went, it was time to get serious about canning and preserving our harvest. Gardening had been work all summer with bugs, weeds, and wet weather. The reward was eating to our heart's content such things as peas, carrots, lettuce, and broccoli along with chard and potatoes.

With a new baby, who demanded night feedings, it was a real pleasure to have the cabin warm, even on the coldest winter nights. On clear, moonlight nights it was not necessary to turn on a light in the cabin as I heated her bottle and fed her. Often, I moved my chair to our large, front room window to watch moose browsing in our yard. I felt tender feelings for these giants of the woods. They symbolized a hardy nature and acceptance of the harsh environment. I felt at peace living in their territory. The moose accepted its life as I did mine.

Winds blew from the northeast, off the Matanuska Glacier and into the Matanuska Valley during the winter. Gusts from 60 to 100 miles per hour were possible. It blew the snow into huge drifts in the woods and on the roads. After one 'blow', I phoned and complained to the Road Commission. It seemed like we were always last to have our road cleared. I was speechless when the receptionist said, "Well, somebody has to be last."

Here we were, at the beginning of our first winter in Alaska, and we never had it so good. We were free from military pressures and snugly comfortable in our little log cabin. Our second child was born healthy and strong. We were contentedly enjoying frontier living. We fell in love with the frozen beauty of Alaska during our first winter. The outdoor winter wonderland, with heavy snow piled high, was a photographer's paradise. The snow-blanketed Chugach Mountains stood out in breath-taking sunset hues of pink and gold. The sky, glacier-ice blue, with scudding clouds added to the magic of this unique country.

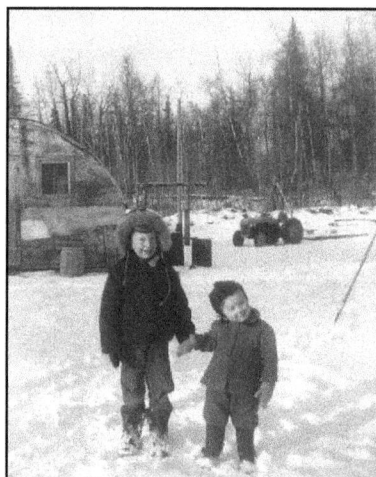

I decided 100 laying hens would put the empty Quonset hut to good use, keep me busy through the winter, and keep us in eggs and meat. The biggest benefit was what I learned about raising chickens.

Bob's parents came to visit soon after we purchased Sawdust, a female Chester White pig that cost $100. The pig became our family pet.

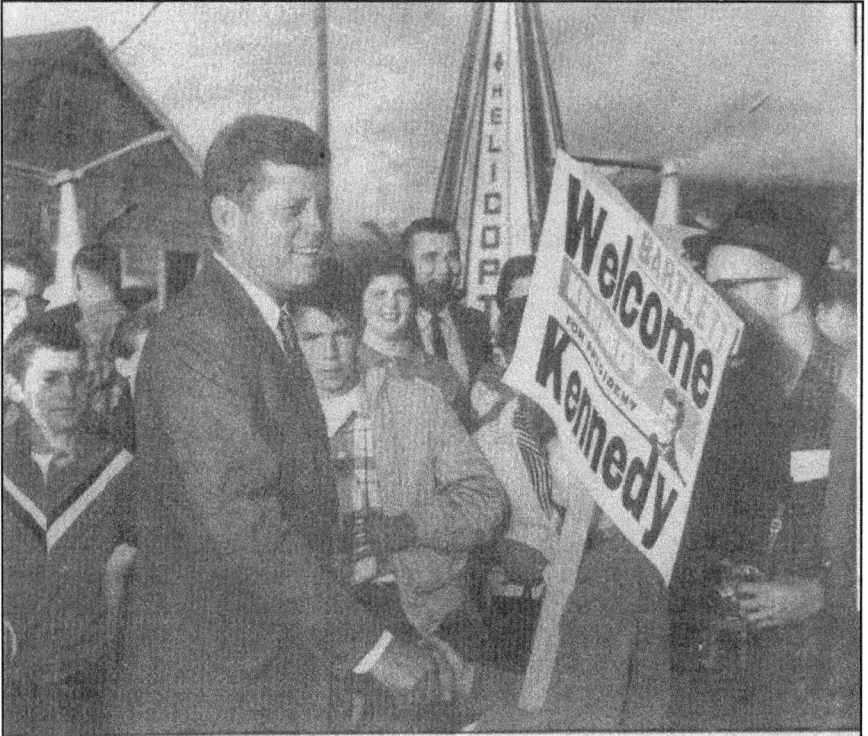

Times file pho

John F. Kennedy, then a U.S. senator from Massachusetts, campaigns at the 1960 Alaska State Fair in Palmer

During the Alaska State Fair in Palmer, Senator John F. Kennedy made his first official campaign speech for the presidency of the United States. He arrived on a bright, sunshiny day, with just a hint of fall in the air. Large crowds sat in the grandstands and waited to hear his speech. The governor and other notables escorted him. Throngs of people were everywhere.

Roger was 10 years old when he landed his first king salmon. The salmon weighed 12 pounds. Without a rod or reel, Roger decided to pelt it with rocks until he could drag it ashore. He brought it home and became an instant hero to his sisters.

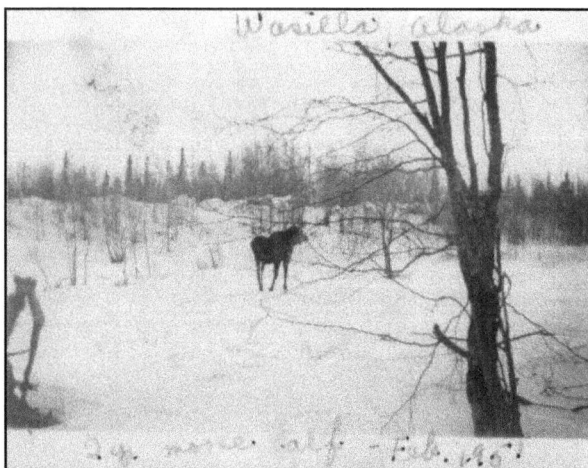

On a cold, winter evening, we were enjoying a quiet time in the living room. One of the kids heard a moose tromping in the snow, close to the house. Bob said to us, as he tiptoed to the door, "Watch this." When the moose got close to the door, Bob flung it open and yelled, "Boo!" The startled moose struck out with his front feet. Bob jumped back into the house, "I almost shook hands with a moose!" We laughed and watched the moose lumber away into the woods.

Winters on the homestead were long, cold, and dark. There weren't many open fields. The forest closed in on the small houses and cabins. Only their distant, twinkling lights through the trees assured warmth.

Friday didn't impress the kids much, and soon they were complaining about him. "Here you have a pony to ride and you're not riding him. Why?" I asked. "We don't, because he won't let us. When Friday gets tired of us on his back, he lays down or scrapes us off against a building or the Volkswagon. He dumps us into mud puddles every chance he gets!"

In 1961, we bought a used Volkswagon bus, originally built as an ambulance. It was empty in the back, except for drawers and cupboards under the beds around the edge. Bob thought it was perfect for hauling feed, tools, and farm supplies. Bob never hated a car so much. He put three rebuilt motors in it, the heater never worked, it drank oil by the quart, and it was hard to start. Bob proclaimed, long and loud, "It's no wonder I can't get along with that Volkswagon. I have a German wife, a German car, and can't cuss in German."

We built a concrete block barn to FHA specifications. Blocks cost 56 cents each. The only thing we did in this building was milk cows. We stored milk in a 250-gallon bulk tank, pumped it into a huge tanker truck for delivery to the processing plant.

After clearing and yanking up roots, we burned the stump rows. Some spring and summer days, the valley air was a hazy-blue with wood smoke. Later, the bulldozer scattered the burned stump rows and restacked the remaining debris to be burned again. This left a large field with no stump row. Cleaning fields could take years.

Open fields were perfect places for those not old enough to get a state driver's license to practice their skills. Linda was not afraid of the big tractor and load of hay. She handled the rig well.

Our dairy was a family operation. Bob and Roger did the muscle work. The girls helped haul bales of hay, herded cows, and fed calves. I was the truck driver and gopher, go for this and go for that—plus chief cook and bottle washer.

Our cows, a motley-looking herd of Jerseys, were a sad sight when they arrived at our farm. Bob and the two drivers unloaded the cows from the truck into the pen. We were stuck with eight Jersey cows that didn't look too promising. At the end of two years, most of them had to be disposed of, because they were such poor producers. We gradually built our herd of 30 cows, with Jersey, Holstein, Guernsey, and Brown Swiss.

A bunker silo is made on top of the ground. Bob made his with two rows of railroad ties stacked on their sides. The sides were 12-feet across at the bottom, and tapered to 16 feet at the top. Pillars braced the ties every five feet. The silo was 50-feet long. Roger and Bob picked up discarded railroad ties along the railroad tracks. This was hard work, but all it cost was muscle power and a truck to bring them home.

Snow could fall at the rate of eight to 10 inches overnight. This hampered dairy activities. We could be snowbound for days at a time.

One night, Bob and I were at a political meeting at the Wasilla School. During a question-and-answer period, a resident asked the speaker about Social Security benefits. The speaker answered, "I can't give you an answer on that. Every time it comes up in the Senate, it's utter confusion." I immediately poked Bob in the ribs and said, "That's the name of our dairy, Udder Confusion!" The name stuck, and soon appeared on a sign at the beginning of our driveway and on our car.

Everyone in the family had to work. Barbara fed calves and Roger worked in the fields with Bob, chopping silage, mowing hay, and twice-a-day, in the milking barn. Linda helped out where she was able. We may not have made any money on the dairy, but the kids learned about good honest work.

Four years after we built our homestead house, we secured a loan to put a full basement under it. In due time, Bob planted a lawn and put up a white-rail fence. I landscaped with annual and perennial flowers. Bob added a porch on the front and the back.

Fall is my favorite time of the year. I admire the golden colors of the shivering leaves, the white clouds overhead, and the frosty, clear nights. Bright moonlight, the fleeting days, and the sense of stillness around our home lent to feeling of fall, along with the satisfaction of a summer's work finished for another year.

The 18, sixth-grade students attended school in Wasilla. In 1959, when Roger attended school, this building was used as a church on Sunday, and as a schoolroom the rest of the week. The school is now located at the Wasilla museum.

LeRoi Heaven, a close friend of Rogers, completed 4H projects by growing vegetables and raising pigs and calves. Roger won a scholarship and two trips for his activities in 4H projects. He went to Chicago and to Washington, D.C.

In 1918, a forest fire swept the Wasilla area. In the open, burned areas, lowbush cranberries grew profusely. A favorite dessert was cooked, sweetened cranberries folded into fresh-whipped cream from our dairy. In the damp, boggy areas of the woods, we found red and black currants, which we used for jelly. Each year, I made at least 50 pints of jams and jellies, which served our yearly needs.

Cabbage left in the gardens until spring became the first easy browse for moose. Long, lanky legs were in the way when the moose tried to reach through the rotting snow to the vegetables. They kneel down to reach their meal.

Buildings were twisted, ruptured, and torn apart. When the great Alaska earthquake was over, it took the city years to rebuild, but business as usual began within two days.

The first time the Plump Stump Sisters performed was in the early sixties at a neighborhood Homemaker's Club Christmas party. Each family was asked to contribute a talent. Three friends, Marj, Mary and Lois said, "Let's form a little group and play something funny."

More Stories

Adam's Apple

Green grass is a cow's favorite food. In the winter, oat and pea silage is also acceptable. To stretch silage until grass is available in the spring, potatoes are a nutritious supplement. We cut potatoes into small pieces, because if not, they could lodge in the cow's throats, causing choking and sometimes death.

Harley, a preacher friend and owner of a much larger dairy operation than ours, lived nearby on Knik Road. As his hay and silage dwindled, he resorted to feeding his cows potatoes.

One day, Harley locked one of his cows in a barn stanchion and, while holding a board on one side of the cow's throat, pounded the other side with a rubber mallet. He thought he was dislodging a whole potato from the cow's throat.

A dairyman friend was nonchalantly leaning against a post, his hands deep in his pockets, enjoying the scene. The friend said to Harley, "What are you doing?" Between hits, Harley tried to explain. "That's no potato, Harley. That's the cow's Adam's apple," commented the friend as he walked from the barn chuckling.

Harley murmured, "It's hard to believe the Lord wanted me to be a farmer."

The friend was my husband, Bob.

Alaska Earthquake

We'd tease Bob often about not feeling minor earthquakes. "Did you feel that one?" I'd say, wild-eyed. Bob would respond calmly, "Didn't feel a thing." It was 5:29 PM on March 27, 1964, the day of the Great Alaska Earthquake—a day I'll never forget.

Roger and Linda had left excitedly for school that morning with permission to stay overnight with friends, something that rarely happened. Roger was with friends nearly 12 miles from the farm. Bob was milking cows, and I had already left my secretarial job in Palmer.

The earthquake struck when I was about four miles from home. The car began to shake like I had a flat tire. As the shaking grew worse, it seemed like all four tires were flat. I decided to stop the car and see what was wrong. As I got out of the car, I had to hang onto the door to keep upright. I realized, fearfully, that my tires were fine and I was in a great quake. The car was jumping up and down on the road. Trees were whipping from side to side, quite often touching the ground. There was a heavy, eerie silence everywhere after the forceful quake subsided.

When the quake was over, I cautiously drove toward home. The ground had been covered with a light skiff of snow. I noticed about every 100 yards, or so, a dark, thin line zigzagged where the road bed had parted or twisted with the violent shaking of the earth.

As I turned into the driveway of our farm, everything looked normal. The only evidence of damage I noticed was the electric and phone lines dangling from the pole in the yard. I quickly turned on the car radio, but only received static. My thoughts whirled as I tried to imagine the severity of the earthquake in places throughout the state.

Bob had been milking cows at the time of the earthquake. He became dizzy while trying to maneuver his way to the nearest step in the milking pit. He noticed the tails of the cows in the milking line were swaying to and fro. The building was also moving from side to side. He thought he was having a heart attack, but soon realized that an earthquake was in progress.

Hurriedly, Bob opened the door of the milking parlor, released the cows, and stumbled his way through the milk room to the outside of the building. The milk in the 250 gallon bulk tank was sloshing from side to side like a giant mixer turned on its highest speed. Milk was escaping from the bulk tank and running down the drain. After he'd made his way outside, he noticed, as I had, the trees were whipping from side to side as they touched the ground with each sweep. The big diesel tractor and the farm truck were each performing a four-legged dance. Bob was expecting them to turn over. They never did. Looking out across the fields he saw the ground was heaving like swells on the ocean. Bob claims it was the longest 5 1/2 minutes he'd ever spent, including the Battle of Midway, during WWII.

Everything was fine in the house. Barbara had held the kitchen cupboard doors shut as best she could during the quake. When it was over, she stood near the back porch door and yelled to her dad, "I'll bet you felt that one, Dad!"

"I felt it! You stay in the house, young lady. See those broken power lines? You could really get hurt."

Several hours later, Bob and I hovered around a small transistor radio and received earthquake reports. The news was grim. As soon as we felt it was safe for travel, we brought Linda home from a nearby neighbor's house. Phones were operating, so we called Roger's host family that evening and found that all was well and brought Roger home the next day.

We settled down after the excitement and discussed our situation. We brought cold milk in from the barn and scrounged fillings for sandwiches.

We went to bed early, moving the girls from their beds in the basement to the couch in the living room. There was a sudden strong after-shock and Linda, who was 10, said, "Mom, is that you turning over in bed?" She was petrified.

From messages on the radio, we knew the electric power would be off for an unknown time, so we set up emergency quarters in the basement. We unhooked the stovepipes of the oil furnace and put an old wood-burning stove, from storage under the stairway, into place. There was plenty of wood stacked in the yard. I kept a tea kettle of water on the stove also a stew simmering in a pot. We were quite comfortable for the next three days.

During these three days, we milked the cows by hand just enough to relieve pressure from their swollen udders. When electricity was restored, we put them back on the electric milkers, no worse for their experience.

Although the damage from the quake was severe in other parts of coastal Alaska, it was exaggerated by the news media. They led us to believe that nearly all of coastal Alaska had been washed away by tidal waves. We also heard that half of Anchorage had fallen into a big hole in the ground. They reported that the Eklutna tunnel bringing the water from the upper lake to the plant below, was blocked, and it could be weeks before electricity would be restored. The truth soon sifted into the news and wasn't nearly as bad as previously thought.

Three weeks later, we spent a day in Anchorage surveying the damage. The Eskimo Scouts, a National Guard Unit, were on duty at businesses to prevent looting. We were awed by Mother nature's force and were thankful none of our family was hurt.

Bears and Sawdust

When we got ready to move onto the homestead, we decided to dress out Sawdust, but still kept a piglet from her third litter to raise for pork for the following winter. Again, Bob built a pig house and fenced yard on the homestead.

That fall, on a dark and rainy night, we heard screeching coming from the pigpen. Bob recognized the sound of a bear trying to get into the pigpen. He grabbed a flashlight and quickly made his way out to the pigpen, but saw nothing.

The next night, we heard the same noise. This time, he grabbed his rifle and ran for the pigpen. Ten-year-old Roger had planted a small patch of potatoes as a 4H project in one end of the garden near the pigpen. That same day, he had hand-dug his potatoes and, in his eagerness, had left huge holes. On the way to the fracas in the pigpen, Bob stumbled in a hole and jammed the end of his rifle into the dirt.

Bob saw a dark shape in the pigpen, recognized it as a bear, and immediately shot. Luckily, the dirt had done no harm to the rifle barrel. It took three shots to kill the bear, but not before the bear killed the pig with his powerful jaws.

Davy Crockett was the popular song then, and it was also Roger's favorite. The following day, Bob dragged the bear into the yard, Roger donned his coonskin cap, and, with Bob's rifle in his hand and one foot on the bear, had his picture taken. Even with our coaxing, Barbara, 7 years old, and Linda 4, wouldn't get near the bear.

Bill Collectors

With babies coming along and various illnesses, we had more hospital bills than we could pay. The hospital was getting impatient, even though we were making minuscule payments now and then. They turned the bill over to a collection agency. Bob was working at the Experimental Farm at the time.

One day, Bob was working with a truck in front of the dairy barn, when a man drove up and said he was looking for a guy named Lincoln.

Bob said, "That's me."

The agent then informed Bob he was working for a collection agency out of an Anchorage office and was there to collect the hospital debt Bob owed. He presented proof of his mission and Bob reluctantly paid him.

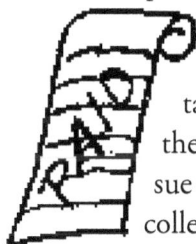

A few days later, we received a letter from the collection agency stating we'd better pay on the bill or they would take us to court. Bob took the next day off work and went to their Anchorage office. He told the manager he was going to sue them for fraud. He then showed the agent the receipt the collector had given him. Immediately, the agent was extra nice and asked Bob to let him see the receipt. Bob said he wouldn't let him put his sticky fingers on the receipt, but would gladly give him a copy of it when he could find a duplicating machine. The agent then said that wouldn't be necessary. He told Bob, that the man who'd made the collection had taken all the money he'd received that day and went south. They honored the receipt even though the money couldn't be recovered.

We also got a notice from the Borough stating our property taxes were delinquent. We took the receipt to the Borough office, informed the manager the bill had been paid and we had a receipt to prove it.

The manager stated, "The Borough's bookkeeping system is infallible and you are wrong. The receipt has the secretary's signature."

The manager called her over to explain. She told him that Bob came to pay it, but only had his paycheck, and they couldn't take a check for more than $100. She said she gave Bob a receipt for taxes owed, told him to cash his check, come back, and pay the taxes. She said Bob never came back.

The three kids and I had waited in the Borough office while Bob cashed his check, returned to pay his taxes, then went home. The manager could see what a lame excuse the secretary gave. In an effort to embarrass Bob, the manager said he would be forced to pay the $157 out of his own pocket.

Bob said, "I'm sorry, but, if I would pay it again, I'd be guilty of paying late and it would go on my record." We never followed through, but imagine the secretary didn't work there very much longer.

Our closest neighbor, Earl Combs, was a member of the Matanuska Electric Association Board of Directors. One evening, he stopped by our house on his way home after a board meeting and said, "If you don't pay your electric bill, MEA will shut your power off."

I went to the file cabinet and pulled out the receipt. The following day, Earl marched down to the MEA office and told the manager the bill had indeed been paid and we had a receipt. He boasted he had stopped by our house and, without knocking, walked in and demanded we pay the bill immediately. When I showed him the receipt, he turned around and walked out.

After a thorough investigation, it came to light that a secretary was using our money for cow feed on her dairy. She always replaced it before the end of the month, but this time the auditors came before she could replace the money. Needless to say, that was her last day of working at MEA. Ever since these fiascoes, Bob has had no use for collection agencies or anyone who worked for them.

A Boy's Summer

One summer day, as I was standing on the bank of Cottonwood Creek near Wasilla, I watched three men vainly trying to catch a salmon.

My mind drifted back to when Roger was a teenager. Roger was our family's only successful fisherman. He had a natural aptitude for catching fish. He had plenty of youth and patience for the sport.

Each May, when school was dismissed for the year, trout fishing ensnared him. Since we lived only 1/2 mile from Cottonwood Creek, shank's mare, as my mother used to call walking, was his means of transportation to and from the fishing hole.

He had staked out in his mind, all likely holes where trout lay, from the little bridge spanning the creek, to the mouth of the creek, two miles downstream.

He spent from five to 10 minutes at each site, and if he didn't catch anything, he moved on. As he worked his way up and down the creek, he caught more trout than any other fisherman. Tourists fishing along the creek, could never figure out how this kid got so many fish.

About the first of August each year, it was standard procedure for Roger to check the creek daily for signs of salmon coming upstream on their annual spawning migration to the upper lakes.One day, Roger and his friend, Billy, were checking the creek. They saw two king salmon swimming upstream just below the Cottonwood Creek bridge.

They lacked fishing gear and had no time to go home for some, so they made do with what they had at hand.

Excitement ran high. At a point near the bridge, the creek narrowed. Each boy gathered a pile of rocks and stacked them near the narrow opening. As the king salmon neared the trap, the boys pelted them with rocks from their stash. When the fish were stunned, the boys waded into the creek, grabbed them by their tails, and dragged them up onto the bank. Each fish weighed about 12 pounds.

Roger figured out the best way to catch a salmon, of course it was legal then, was to use a 1 1/2-inch snag hook and wrap solder around the shank, giving it plenty of weight.

He tied chalk line to a willow pole. The best length for a willow pole was one a little taller than the boy. The line, attached to the pole, had to be long enough to reach across the creek from the bank. Roger and Clark, John Lemon's son, securely braced the fishing poles to their chests. They threw the hook into the water near the opposite bank and slowly pulled it back across the creek until it was near the fish they were attempting to catch. They yanked hard on the line, snagged the salmon, and quickly tossed it onto the bank. The salmon didn't have a chance to fight, and it didn't scare other fish.

As salmon season progressed, local fishermen and tourists lined the creek banks. Some families arrived with their campers and tents for extended periods of time.

During the week, most of the luckless fishermen consisted of women and children. The men had to return to town to work all week. Very few salmon were caught.

Inexperienced fishermen at the creek became an interesting spectacle for the boys. They bribed the boys with quarters to catch fish for them. The fishermen and the boys both thought they were getting a super deal. Everyone was happy.

The boys deliberately tried to snag salmon that already had hooks imbedded in their bodies. They also tried to recover the hooks and lures snagged in trees and bushes. When water levels were low, they reclaimed hooks and lures laying on the creek bottom. They polished and repainted, and then displayed them on a flannel board in an attractive manner. They sold them to the fishermen for half-price. Roger and Clark had as many as 100 hooks and lures at a time on their display board.

No one could understand why these two boys wasted their time collecting hooks and lures. When the salmon were running, and the fishermen had lost their hooks and lures, they didn't want to take the time to go back to Wasilla to buy more. They gladly paid the price for used hooks and lures displayed by two energetic boys. This proved to be a very lucrative business.

While standing in line at a sporting goods store in Anchorage, Bob and I overheard a customer ahead of us tell the clerk about the kids at Cottonwood Creek who were reselling hooks and lures and serving snacks to the fishermen.

Some fishermen were too finicky to clean their fish, or didn't know how, so the boys charged 25 cents a fish to take care of this messy chore. They had a system worked out where they cleaned a fish in less than a minute while tourists watched in awe, cameras flashing.

One year, Roger used the farm tractor and hay wagon to set up a portable restaurant at the creek. He bought pop by the case, made coffee on a propane stove, and stocked candy bars and hot dogs.

Campers who pulled too far off the road and into mud near the creek, often became stuck. Roger used the tractor and charged $5 for towing service, adding the money to his rapidly growing savings account.

He made signs and stapled them on the outside of the wagon:

VOTE FOR I. M. SMELLY—THE FISHERMAN'S FRIEND

VOTE FOR DUE NUTTIN—OUR MAN FOR THE LEGISLATURE

GET STINKIN WITH LINCOLN

VOTE FOR I. KETCHUM—DOG CATCHER

ROBEM, CHEATUM, AND BURNEM—LAWYERS

When the boys weren't fishing, they spent uncounted hours at the culvert near the bridge on Cottonwood Creek. The force of the water from upstream carried them, yelling and screaming, swiftly through the culvert and out the other side. One thing Roger vividly remembers is that he caught the dickens when he arrived home from wading in the creek with his new shoes.

The local 4H Club, of which Roger and Barbara were members, placed two, 50-gallon drums near the parking lot to be used as garbage containers. Once a week, Roger emptied the garbage containers in our own private dump on the farm.

The 4H members made a scarecrow with tin cans and wire and placed it beside the garbage cans. They made a sign requesting the cooperation of everyone to help keep the surrounding area neat and clean. In the two years Roger was involved with his business venture at the creek, he cleared $400. He banked it all for college.

He also earned $300 hiring out as a farm hand to neighboring farmers. This money, coupled with two scholarships awarded for his 4H projects and two summer jobs with the State Highway Department, helped finance two years of college.

Bread Making

Making bread was never one of my talents. During my first summer in Alaska, I thought I should learn how to make bread. Cookbooks weren't much help. Explanations for making bread were altogether different from what I remembered from my younger years.

The cookbook said to "knead thoroughly." I've seen bread poked, shaped, slapped, and massaged into beautiful works of art. Mine collapsed—overdone on the outside, underdone on the inside, resembling pale blobs not fit for man or beast.

I tossed the rejects out to the birds, but they would have no part of them. Treating the loaves like rocks, they tried to sharpen their beaks on them. Even when soaked in water, my bread wasn't palatable—not even to our half-grown, ever-hungry dog.

Twice a week for the next month or so, my futile attempts were the same. I was determined to bake bread that looked as delicious as the pictures in the cookbook. Memories of the taste and smell of fresh bread just out of the oven also encouraged me.

At every opportunity gleaned from my busy daily life, I watched friends and neighbors make bread. I asked questions of these experts and com-

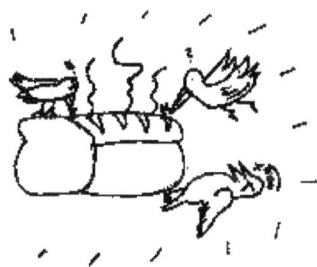

plained about my ignorance. After weeks of dogged effort, I could see some improvement. We ate the bread the same day it came out of the oven, and maybe on the second. After that, it was again inedible. Eventually, I produced fairly light, crusty, golden-brown loaves of sweet-smelling bread. Every member of the family begged for it as soon as it came from the oven. After the kids grew up, they said one of their fondest memories was coming home from school on dark, cold, winter days to a brightly-lit home filled with the aroma of fresh bread.

When the kids were teenagers, four loaves of bread and a large pan of cinnamon rolls I baked every three days didn't stretch until the next baking day. To supplement bread, I made baking powder biscuits.

I often threatened to get our neighbor's recipe for her bread. In those days, during my occasional stays at the local hospital, Elaine did her neighborly duty and brought over a loaf of her fresh bread. She always delivered it, along with sympathy, on the first day I was in the hospital, and the family was still eating the same loaf of bread when I returned a few days later.

Upon my arrival home, I asked Bob, "Why don't you guys eat Elaine's bread like you eat mine?"

He answered, "Her bread tastes OK, but it's heavy. If I eat a slice, it just sinks to the bottom of my belly and sits there."

Numerous times, during my first attempts, I asked Bob, "Is my bread getting any better?"

The only answer I got from him was, "Well, I ate it, didn't I?"

Now, he says, "When are you going to make bread again? I hate store-bought bread." I figured with that request, I'd finally mastered the art of making bread.

Dog Team

Wenter Harvey, a preacher from Wasilla, was concerned about driving a dog team. He couldn't get them to 'Gee' or 'Haw' for him, and they were uncontrollable most of the time.

He sought professional advice from a friend of his, Ilah Senske, an educated lady who was a salty character with rough language. She'd carried mail, by dog team, from Wasilla to Independence Mine, so was acquainted with controlling a dog team.

Wenter said to her, "How do you get your dogs to move when you want them to?"

Ilah put her hands on her hips, took a deep breath, and shouted in the loudest voice she could muster, "Get up you sons-a-bitches!"

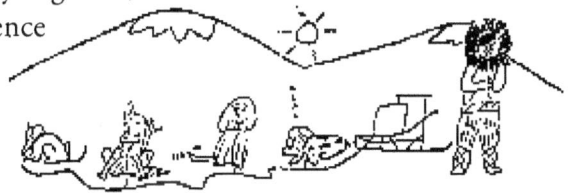

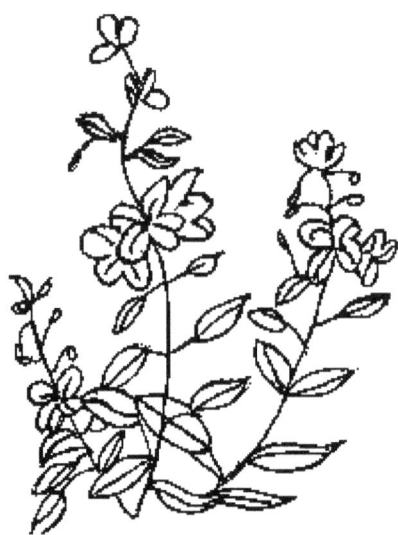

Fall, My Favorite Time

The long days of summer flew by, and we were so busy that we welcomed the first fall frost with a sigh of relief. Fall's my favorite time of year. I admire the golden colors of the shivering leaves, the white clouds overhead, and the frosty, clear nights. Honking geese heading south and the hooting of the owls during the quiet nights were nostalgic and seemed to make me hurry in preparations for the cold winter ahead. Our home, snug and cozy, showered with occasional cold, rainy days, kept me indoors straightening shelves and starting new sewing projects.

We welcomed various forms of wildlife at the farm. Our constant visitors were owls, foxes, and squirrels, and we watched them build nests and gather food for the coming winter. Bright moonlight, the fleeting days, and the sense of stillness around our home, lent to the feeling of fall, along with the satisfaction of a summer's work finished for another year.

GI Schooling

Since almost every homesteader was a veteran of WWII, he or she was eligible for on-the-farm training, a program to aid veterans in making their living on their farmsteads. A provision of the program was that a veteran had to make a living from their acreage. They automatically became disqualified if they accepted employment away from the farm. The Veterans Administration held classes every Tuesday night at the grade school in Wasilla.

As I was a Navy veteran of WWII and didn't work off the farm, I was eligible for this program. Bob was bringing home a steady paycheck from his job at the MVFCA and, though he also was a veteran, he was not eligible for this class. Attendance in class entitled you to a $100-a-month subsistence check. This small stipend gave each person who attended the class a reason to stay on their homestead and make it work, without seeking employment elsewhere. Our monetary gift paid the grocery and gas bills and kept us in shoes, boots, and clothing our growing family demanded.

I eagerly looked forward to this Tuesday night out. It was my event of the week. While I attended the one-hour class, Herb and Jewell Holstein's daughter, Ruby, took care of the kids, and Bob waited in the car. Week after week, I listened to the teacher talk about pigs. He told how and what to feed them. He talked about sheltering, diseases and breeding problems. When he discussed the breeding habits and problems of pigs, he fidgeted, turned pink and stumbled through explanations. I felt sorry for him. He was more embarrassed with a woman in his class than I ever was by listening to him. This windfall lasted only a few months, though, and by late, fall the classes were disbanded due to lack of government funds. As always, all good things come to an end.

Go to Hell

On a sunny, calm day Bob was tuning up the tractor. A man and a woman in a fancy car drove into our yard. Any car in better shape than our Studebaker pickup truck, with its tail gate gone, rattley fenders, cracked windows, and dents, was a fancy car.

Bob imagined the richly dressed man and woman were looking for Cottonwood Creek. The salmon were running and Bob assumed the strangers were going fishing.

The driver said, "Is this the right road?"

This irked Bob and he retorted, "If you're going to hell it is!"

The man was upset, the woman was laughing. They drove off in a huff.

Kennedy's Mud Hole

During the Alaska State Fair in Palmer, Senator John F. Kennedy made his first official campaign speech for the presidency of the United States. He arrived on a bright, sunshiny day with just a hint of fall in the air. Large crowds at the grandstands waited to hear his speech. The governor and other notables escorted him. Throngs of people were everywhere.

Ten rows of folding chairs had been set up in front of the grandstand where Kennedy was to speak.

Herb Holstein was on the Democratic Party Committee. He had 30 complimentary tickets for these seats and gave them out to constituents. Bob and I, two of his chosen friends, had ring-side seats and felt honored to be there.

Kennedy was a handsome man; youthful, pleasant, friendly and not the least bit conceited. He displayed the ability of someone able to handle duties of the presidency.

Rain had fallen on the previous three days. The unpaved fairgrounds were muddy. Just inside the gates of the fairgrounds, as his entourage entered, a mud hole stopped the presidential candidate's car in its tracks. People jumped to their aid from behind barriers. They pushed the presidential car out of the mire, and the festivities continued as planned.

When Kennedy's speech was over, he mingled with the crowd. We were close to him, and, consequently, I took the opportunity to get his autograph. I handed Senator Kennedy my program, and he hurriedly scrawled his name. Many other people had the same idea and did the same as I did.

Years later, I wrote to an autograph club inquiring about the value of his signature. They wanted to purchase it for $100. I didn't accept their offer. To this day, few believe I have his autograph.

Kids

All too soon, the kids were grown. It seemed they were babies one year and teenagers the next. I'll have to admit, there were times when we wondered if they would ever grow up. I was known as the meanest mother in the world, until they met two other mothers who were meaner. I never got delegated lower than the third-meanest mother in the world. They were convinced I had eyes in the back of my head. I convinced them they were right.

There was nothing wrong with their appetites, and they brimmed over with boundless energy. They skimmed the cream from the milk stored in the milking barn, and drank it whenever they got the chance. They stole half-filled pea pods by the pocketful from the garden and retreated to the back of the house to eat them, far out of range of my watchful eyes, or so they thought. When they picked berries, they canned more berries by eating them in the berry patch than they put in the bucket.

They complained, "We know when it's summer. All we get is salmon and rhubarb!"

They insisted they were the only kids who had to work. They herded cows, picked up rocks and roots from newly cleared fields, and stacked bales of hay. They tracked mud on clean floors, fought while doing dishes, and were absolutely exhausted after weeding only one row in the garden. They complained about homework and grumbled about going to bed. They peeled potatoes thick and wondered why we were always out of them. I constantly reminded them about the waste and told them to just peel the peelings, not the potatoes.

They threw empty tin cans into the snow near the house. They claimed they were afraid of the moose that bedded down near the garbage cans. In the spring they protested loud and long when they had to pick up the same tin cans. As teenagers, they hired out as baby-sitters and worked well for neighbors. They mowed lawns and shoveled snow, took out ashes, split and carried wood. Their bedrooms were a disaster.

It took all summer to teach them to leave the doors open and all winter to teach them to leave the doors shut.

They never had a thing to wear. They moaned, "How come all the other kids get to go places whenever they want and we don't?" "How come we're the only kids in school who wear patched jeans?"

They made their entertainment by collecting frogs and keeping them in the cow watering tank. They thought eating raw rhubarb would give them instant strength. They were on time for meals, but hastily disappeared to their playhouse in the woods or out to see what Dad might be up to when there were dishes to wash. They were active in 4H projects.

The kids understood any animals we might acquire were not pets. If they became pets, they had to be useful as well. Dogs were kept for protection and to assist in herding cows, cats to keep the rodent population under control. Geese, turkeys, and chickens were for meat and eggs. We sold extra eggs or traded them for groceries at the local grocery store. We kept a hog for meat and cows for meat and milk.

The kids had the usual childhood diseases: mumps, chicken pox, and several kinds of measles. Parents thought it wise to expose their children to these diseases, rather than get an unexpected surprise. Of all the diseases, polio was the most terrifying. Parents, including us, made their children stay away from the public beaches or swimming holes in the summer. We were grateful when a polio vaccine was developed. Free shots were dispensed once a month until a series of three was complete, thus guaranteeing immunity.

Due to lack of sanitation, many children came to school with lice, ringworm, or impetigo. I heated water on the stove for bathing and made sure our kids were clean, so they were never infected. Children with impetigo used a special purple soap. A knit cap containing disinfectant was used to treat ringworm. The public health nurse came around to the homes regularly. The kids recognized her gray carryall. When she drove in the yard, they scattered. They knew they were going to get a shot of some sort. Hiding never worked because I found them.

Roger had an experience with food that he'll never forget. Bob, the girls, and I went Outside on a trip. Roger had complete charge of the dairy, including milking the cows. One evening, he decided to make himself some rice for supper. He put rice in a medium-sized kettle with lots of water, then left to do the milking. When he got back in the kitchen a few hours later, rice was running down the front of the stove and collecting in piles on the floor.

About that time, Barbara, a curious five-year-old, climbed a tall birch tree at the edge of our yard. The wind began blowing fiercely. We don't know how long she clung to the swaying branch, but Bob happened to see her. He knew he was too heavy to go up after her, so he stood in the wind yelling explicit instructions, as only Bob could do, on how to get down. As usual, she didn't panic or get excited.

Our meat supply dwindled to almost nothing a number of times. I remember loudly complaining to Bob, "If you don't do something soon about our meat supply, we're going to have to eat the cats." Goodness knows, we had plenty of them around the farm. A few evenings later, as I served homemade soup to the family, Linda sat in her place at the table, slowly stirring her soup. She woefully looked up at me and asked timidly, "Is this cat soup?"

Barbara, as a teenager, had a bread-baking project for 4H. She didn't do too well. One day, I came home from work early and caught her dumping the bread dough into the snowbank beside the house. She told me it was such a disaster she had to start over and she thought I wouldn't know the difference if she got rid of the first attempts before I arrived home.

That summer I phoned from work and asked her to make a cake for supper. She said to me, "What kind?"

I told her, "Whatever kind you want. Just pick out one you like."

When I got home and opened the door to the kitchen, there was a slow-moving mass coming from the oven door. "They must have made a mistake in the factory." Barbara explained. "I picked out an angel food cake mix. The factory put two packages in the box, so I fixed one according to the directions and I threw the other one in the garbage."

That same summer she wanted to make a rhubarb pie. She rolled out the crust and lined the pie pan. No problem. She put three cups of cut up rhubarb in the crust and put it in the oven for an hour. When she took the pie out, it looked awful. Each piece of rhubarb was as hard as a bullet. She had forgotten to put eggs, sugar, moisture, or thickening in the rhubarb before putting it in the oven. For many years, we teased her, trying to get her to make the family another rhubarb pie.

The girls were always busy with their two dogs, many cats, and an assortment of dolls who demanded lots of tender loving care.

The two collie dogs, Lassie and Ranger, were as different as day and night. Lassie was quiet and gentle, very protective. Ranger, her son, was rambunctious and untrainable. Ranger never learned to avoid porcupines. Bob often saw Ranger cowering and whining near the barn, evidently in severe pain. His face would be full of quills that had to be removed, one at a time, with pliers. Barbed much like a fish hook, quills can work themselves inward until they are totally imbedded. If not removed quickly, can even cause death if they reach a vital organ.

Roger loved to tease the girls unmercifully—throwing cats in mud puddles just to hear the girls scream, or chasing them with bugs. However, he was fearlessly protective of them when anyone outside the family was teasing or mistreating them.

The girls complained they never had any dolls. One day, I counted 12 dolls laying in a row across Bob's big, wooden plywood tool box on the back porch. Some lacked arms. Some were without legs or hair. The girl's love and imagination didn't notice. They spent many hours dressing and undressing their dolls. They did the same with some cats, and wheeled them around the yard in their doll buggy. The girls were just as happy with an old, faded baby blanket as they were with a new doll blanket made out of scraps of colorful fabric.

One hectic day, Bob came into the porch, roughly brushed the dolls onto the floor in a big heap, opened his tool box, grabbed his tools, and marched out the door to his task. The girls were overwhelmed at his thoughtlessness. I saw how the girls were devastated.

I marched out the door and called to him, "Bob, do you have any idea how you hurt the girls' feelings? They treat those dolls like real babies. Next time just tell them to move the dolls."

He answered, "Okay. Okay!" Bob kept his word.

One Salmon

With Roger gone to college, it was Bob's and my responsibility to get enough salmon to last the winter. Cottonwood Creek had been fished extensively, so we looked elsewhere for a place to catch our supply of salmon.

"We're going to Copper Center and go up the river. No one else fishes there," Bob exclaimed repeatedly.

One day, we loaded up the back of the pickup truck with all manner of camping gear, fishing equipment, rainwear, and food. With complete faith in catching a year's supply of salmon, we traveled to Copper Center, where fishing had been excellent on the Copper River.

After parking in a campground, we asked at the local sporting goods store about renting a riverboat and operator for the next day. The skipper of the boat was to deliver us to a spot where he promised us salmon success. We agreed on a fee. At 6 o'clock the next morning, we were ready. The 20-minute boat trip upriver through the fast water, dodging huge boulders and sandbars, was most enjoyable. We land-lubbers put our complete faith and trust in the skill of our guide.

With our lunches and fishing gear, and a promise of a pick-up at 5 o'clock, he left us on a gravel bar. We were excited about a good day of fishing. We were residents, so we qualified to use dip-nets. We fished for hours and, finally, Bob netted one salmon.

We watched a tourist with rod and reel, walk a great distance along the riverbank on the opposite shore of our gravel bar. In less than 20 minutes he had six fat salmon on his stringer. Six was his limit and we could hear him shouting as he raced back to tell his friends of his good fortune. He brought them back to his lucky spot across from us. It didn't take long for his friends to get their limit. They were deliriously happy as they walked back to their camp. We sat on the gravel bar, with one fish, hordes of mosquitoes, and the threat of a rainstorm hovering above.

One Fish, Again

The following summer, we had another luckless fishing trip. I had submitted my name to the Pepsi Cola Company in Anchorage, and won a three-day, all-expense-paid, fly-in fishing trip. The prize was for two people to Lake Iliamna, located on the west side of Cook Inlet, about two hours flying time by bush plane from Anchorage.

Our plane trip to the lodge was perfect. Slivers of late afternoon sunlight sifted through misty clouds. Hundreds of little islands dotted the north end of the lake. There was tundra as far as the eye could see.

After a smooth landing, we signed for our room and enjoyed a standing rib roast dinner. We arranged with our fishing guide for a 7 o'clock departure the next morning to the fishing grounds. Rainwear and rubber boots were necessary attire of the day.

In a nearby small, native settlement, bright red fillets of salmon hung from drying racks at the lake's edge. Children and yapping dogs were playing around small, tar-paper shacks. Small fishing boats balanced in the sand at water's edge.

We stood in a misty rain and fished for over six hours before our guide decided the fish weren't biting. We returned to the lodge in defeat with scowls on our faces, stomachs hungry, and chilled to the bone.

We spent the rest of the afternoon reading, sleeping, and resting. The next morning, a torrential rain was falling. We made no attempt to go fishing. The skies cleared to a small degree by late afternoon, and we picked a gallon of blueberries near the lodge.

The third day, it was still cloudy and drippy, but restlessness sent us out into the boat again. I hooked a large lake trout but it got away as I was about to bring it into the boat. Again, we came back to the lodge, wet, tired, hungry—and skunked.

The next day, we were to depart, but the plane couldn't land due to heavy rain. We picked another gallon of blueberries, got acquainted with the cook, and played cards with other guests.

Late in the afternoon, a chartered float plane with two hunters aboard landed near the lodge. Our host made a quick deal with the pilot to deliver us to Anchorage. We had five minutes to get to the plane. We grabbed our gear, not forgetting the two gallons of blueberries from the cook's freezer, and ran for the plane.

The sun was making one last feeble attempt to shine. I must say the two-hour flight was the most enjoyable trip either one of us have ever had. The countryside was still a vibrant green. Mists rising, trees glistening with dew, an occasional moose browsing in the woods, and the sun's rays setting on the mountain tops was astounding. As we flew through two mountain valleys, we were in another world.

All too soon we were in Anchorage and on our way to Wasilla. If our calculations were correct, our two gallons of blueberries cost the Pepsi Cola Company $850. The only money we spent was $7 for a bright-red sweatshirt with Lake Iliamna stamped on the front.

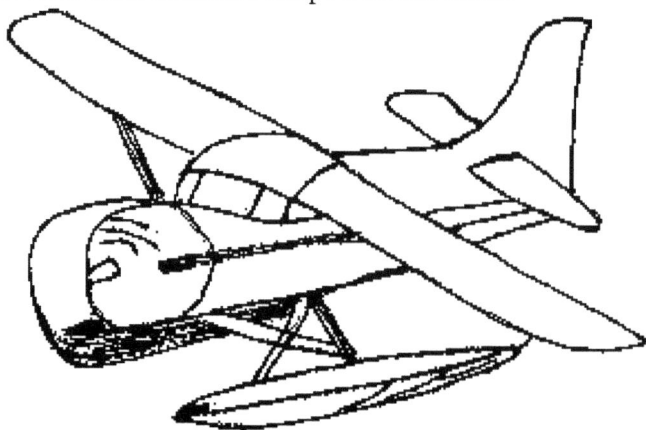

Over the Hill

In 1956, when Alaska was still a territory, two men went berserk, raped a Wasilla woman, ransacked some cabins, and stole rifles.

To make a long story short, the community formed a posse to search for the two criminals. Armed with rifles, and organized by the Territorial Police, they met at the Police Station in Palmer. Harold Newcomb and Bob paired up for the search. They were warily crawling through a small meadow overgrown with high native grass, when suddenly they heard the click of a rifle bolt. They immediately dropped to the ground and stayed put. The criminals were captured in a nearby potato field. The outlaws were turned over to the Territorial Police, received a trial, and were sent to jail.

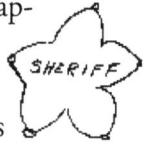

This was an example of how we took care of some criminals in those days. We sure couldn't see that happening today, although we both believe there would be less crime if the local people took care of it themselves.

Sawmill,
Sourdough Style

A neighbor, Bill Senske, and his wife, Ilah, lived a simple, independent life. Like most old-timers, he detested modern conveniences, fought electricity and TV for many years before succumbing to them. In his later years, however, he became a real couch potato, watching TV from morning to night.

During his working years, he had a job as a machinist at Independence Gold Mine, near Hatcher Pass, east of Wasilla. At his home, he rigged up a sawmill to run off water power from Cottonwood Creek. Bill rigged the saw with a one-tooth blade. He put a log on the carriage, set the saw, put it in gear, and went to work. When he got home in the evening, one board would be sawed through. He set it again in the evening. Another board was ready the next morning. He sawed enough lumber in this manner to build his house and outbuildings.

Sourdough in Prison

In the late 1950s, I read a story of a sourdough who went to Anchorage in December. He threw rocks through the windows of Penney's Department Store, then stood waiting the reaction he knew would happen. Soon, the police came and arrested him. The judge sentenced him to 90 days in jail. This same incident took place year after year. Finally, the judge, in his wisdom, realized the sourdough was breaking the windows on purpose so he could spend 90 days in jail during the worst part of winter.

He said to the sourdough, "Thirty days."

The sourdough became upset and said to the judge, "You always give me 90 days. If you give me 30 days, I'll have to go back to my cabin, cut wood, melt ice for water, and do my own cooking."

The Bus Driver

Bob and I periodically heard about the school bus driver from our three kids. For seven years, Claude, commonly called Clod, was the bus driver on their route. He became a regular topic of conversation in our house. He informed every child on the bus he was the big honcho and everyone had to do what he told them, without hesitation.

The kids ignored him or laughed at him behind his back. Every so often, he stopped the bus, slowly got out of his seat, turn around, put his hand on the ceiling, lean over the support bar, and threatened, "All right, you kids. Settle down or I'll throw you off the bus."

He made a dramatic production out of his threats. He once was a police officer in Texas, and he knew all about cops and told the students on his bus they were starting out to be criminals. Everyone sat quietly and listened. As soon as he got back into his seat, everyone went back to their usual mischief. Our trio said it got to be fun to bait him about being a cop.

Most of the kids were rowdy and liked to holler and yell on the bus, the way kids usually do. Originally, they weren't out to deliberately harass him, but Claude pretended they were. He'd fake getting upset. Then the kids would really harass him.

Generally, he was considered a pretty good guy. He never scolded anyone that didn't have it coming. He pointed out to the boys, who were about 12 years old, that they were all grown men and should act like men. He did the same thing with the girls. They had to act like young ladies.

One day, when the kids were giving him a particularly bad time, he gave them one of his lectures. His lecturing began: "Now you kids better stop throwing papers all over the floor or you won't have the privilege of eating on the bus. I'll just take all your privileges away. And you big kids, you watch the little kids and see that they don't get out of hand. If they do, turn around and thump them." Contradicting himself, he continued, "If I see any big kids hitting the little ones, you're going to be in big trouble."

There were times when the bus got stuck in snowdrifts and was late picking up the kids. Roger, Barbara, and Linda, waited for him a reasonable length of time. When they got thoroughly chilled, they'd retreat to the house to get warm. When the bus finally came, they'd run out to the road as fast as they could. Claude would inevitably growl, "Well, well. Couldn't you kids get up this morning?"

On the last day of the school year, Claude gave the kids Hershey bars. Then he would take them to the NIKE site at the very end of his route, where the GI's provided more goodies for the kids. When the fun was over, Claude took everyone home by reversing the route—all the kids getting off first all year got to see what it was like getting off last. This was a thrill for a bus load of excited kids.

One winter, when the snow was abnormally deep, a cow moose making her winter home in the woods across the road from our house chased the school bus daily. Between the harassment of our dogs and the intrusion of the orange monster that wheeled down the road twice a day, the moose became very hostile. Her antics got so bad some mornings, Bob took his 30.06 and escorted the kids to the bus stop. Bob, the kids, and the moose survived the winter.

Tooth and Tire

All my life, I've been plagued with bad teeth. The worst time I had was the year after Barbara was born. I had the dentist pull my teeth, one by one, as the pain became unbearable. At this time, I was learning how to drive the pickup truck. Bob was working at the MVFCA in Palmer and left for work about 7:30 AM and returned about 6 PM.

I made an appointment at the dentist and the only time I could get was noon on a Thursday. How was I to get there? I wouldn't ask neighbors, as they were busy with their own work. I talked Jewel into taking four-year-old Roger and eight-month-old Barbara for a few hours while I kept the appointment.

This was the first time I'd driven the pickup by myself. Early in the morning all four of us went to Palmer, left Bob off at his job, and returned home. By 11 o'clock, I took the kids to the Holsteins, drove to Palmer, had my tooth pulled, and drove home. About five miles from home I had a hard time keeping the truck on the road. I blamed it on the rough gravel and my lack of experience.

When I came to the Holsteins driveway, Herb came running out of the house with a pail of water. He doused the rear tire and the steam shot high into the air.

He said, "I saw you down the road, trailing smoke. I knew you had a flat tire. I could tell by the way you were driving."

I got out of the truck and looked at the smoking back tire. Steam from the water, almost obscured my vision. The tire was bent and twisted like a licorice stick. The inside fibers were sticking out like an old man's whiskers. The rim was scarred from the road gravel.

"I was suffering from the tooth extraction and probably wasn't too alert," I meekly said. Herb just shook his head. "Besides, what could I have done anyway? I don't know how to change a tire. Come on Herb, Take me home. My face hurts me!"

Bob wasn't too happy with me that evening, but didn't say much when he saw my bruised and swollen face. He chalked the incident up to inexperience and, when I was well, showed me how to recognize and change a flat tire.

Lincoln Said

Roger wrote in his journal, the things my father used to say.
If I knew the answer to that question I wouldn't be a farmer.
You kids must think I'm made of money.
I wouldn't have dared to say that to my dad.
You're my right hand man.
I couldn't make a down payment on a free meal.
I ought to tan your hide.
Do you want to grow up to be a ditch digger?
You kids ask me too many questions.
Maybe someday you kids will learn.

He also wrote, the things my mother used to say.
You kids don't have enough work to do.
Go to sleep or I'll rock you to sleep.
You kids are turning into assets instead of liabilities.
If you don't find something to do I'll find you something.
Get outside and help your dad.
Do I have to repeat it again?
The Navy, Marines, or Army would straighten you out.
If you can't hear maybe you can feel.
Be useful as well as ornamental.

Rhubarb Wine

Jack lived in a small cabin across the street from the Wasilla School. The cabin had few comforts and a dirt floor. Jack had sailed all over the world in windjammers. There wasn't anything of practical value he didn't know.

He had a job at Fort Richardson, building large warehouses. He knew more about putting up large steel trusses than the well educated engineers. He told the engineers to get out of his way and he would get some Wasilla boys to help him put the trusses in place.

True to his word, he did just that. He was proud of himself as he hammered the first rivet in place, proving to the engineers he knew what he was talking about.

Waldo and Bob visited Jack one night. Jack was in good spirits when the men arrived at his humble abode. He'd just opened a bottle of his homemade rhubarb wine. Bob had a drink, then another. The wine slid down easy. Bob could talk fine and didn't feel woozy, but the feeling went out of his face and down one side. He never drank Jack's wine again.

Jack had a smart, little cocker spaniel. Bob had left the door open when he came into Jack's cabin that evening. Jack told the dog to shut the door. The dog made a run for the door, hit it with his front paws, and slammed it shut. Jack talked to his dog, and Bob swore that dog understood every word he said. The dog was Jack's only companion. Consequently, they communicated well together.

In the early 50s, Jack won the Nenana Ice Classic, a lottery on the day, hour, month, and minute the ice starts to move on the Nenana River in the spring. A tripod set up in the middle of the river trips a clock on shore which records the exact time. In those days the payoff was about $10,000.

Back then the IRS didn't take taxes out of the winnings. It was the winner's responsibility to pay taxes on the windfall. Paying taxes on his winnings was the least of Jack's concerns. He loaned money to anyone who gave him a hard-luck story. He was continually buying rounds of drinks at the local bar. His generosity at the bar was a weakness that drained his billfold.

April 15 came and went. Jack couldn't pay his taxes. The IRS kept warning him to pay up.

Finally, two agents came to his cabin to collect.

One agent said, "Jack, we're going to have to take your cabin for the overdue taxes."

Jack waved his arm around, pointing to the single room and it's contents and said, "There it is, take it."

Both agents rolled their eyes, and with a sigh of defeat, left the premises. Jack beat the IRS, and they never bothered him again.

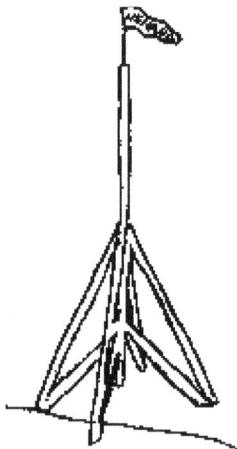

Neighbors and Friends

We readily adapted to life in the North. Our friends ranged from alcoholics to preachers, each for what they had to offer. Neighbors were great; you could borrow a cup of flour, sugar, or even a stepladder from them.

There were no Jones' to keep up with—we borrowed from Mr. Jones, who was the banker. We admired each other's gardens. Canned goods, proudly displayed in neat rows in cellars and cupboards were conversation pieces. We discussed food prices and headlines, weather, and latest gossip, whether we agreed or disagreed.

Gandy Dancing

When the cows went to their new home, Bob went to work for the Alaska Railroad, thinking it would be only for a day. The earthquake had caused a great deal of damage to the tracks along the Matanuska River, about eight miles east of Palmer. One day on the job ended up being two days.

The track was bent out of shape and washed out in places. The men put down new track where needed, graded the bed again, tamped ties in place, and raised the track in sunken sections. Repairs were needed to help get the coal mines at Eska and Jonesville running again. The military at Fort Richardson and Elmendorf Air Force Base used the coal for power and heat.

None of the men knew when they went to work the first morning, that they wouldn't be able to go home again for two days. Most had brought lunch for an eight-hour shift. The railroad fed them one meal after 16 hours of gandy dancing. They ate at the Matanuska Hotel in Palmer, where the section foreman's wife was running the hotel dining room. The men were famished. They ate like the farmers most of them were: mashed potatoes, gravy, steak, salad, vegetables, and pie—and all they could eat. The Alaska Railroad paid the bill. From then on, the same restaurant sent sandwiches out to them. When this special job was finished, Bob continued to work on other jobs for the railroad during the next five months.

The section foreman, Walt Gryski, was a small, neat man known to us as Little Lord Fauntleroy. He loved to play poker. At noon, the men ate in one of the railroad tool shacks. They'd get Walt into a poker game and allow him to win a bit, and then Walt would allow the men to take two hours for lunch.

On the job, Walt would pick an easy target and pester him almost unmercifully. He'd find a sensitive or weak area of any man and tease him, pick on him, and say degrading things about him to others. It turned out that Bob got along with Walt very well because he could take his derogatory remarks and return his continuous banter. Walt kept Bob on the job as long as he could.

When freeze-up came, and white Termination Dust started falling, Bob was laid off. He was considered temporary hire. Bob really liked this job, as hard as it was, because most of the men on the gang were good people. A hard-work job usually attracts good people who roll with the punches.

At the time of his layoff, the freight depot needed extra help. They hired Bob to help deliver parts, furniture, machinery, groceries, and other freight to retail merchants around the Palmer area. He didn't have much to do on this job, with no freight to deliver on some days. The job lasted until about February 1965.

Gardening and Harvesting

My hoarding instinct comes forward in autumn, and I'm most happy when putting up jelly, jams, pickles, fruit, and vegetables for winter. Somehow, I have the idea that it gives me security from the cold of the long winter, like putting money in the bank. After harvesting, we turned our thoughts to putting improvements on our home. Short days and cold weather did not hinder making improvements in our home.

Roger's Enterprise

The summer of 1960, when Roger was 13 years old, he tried his first big venture into the world of free enterprise. He needed a 4H project and decided to go into the potato business. He talked his dad into letting him use 1/2 acre of land. It was an irregular part of a forage field, so it didn't cause too much inconvenience.

Roger kept accurate records, an important part of 4H work. He borrowed the necessary amount of fertilizer from Bob and agreed to pay him when the crop was sold. He obtained the necessary seed from Ted Knutson by making the same agreement to pay when the crop sold. Then, he borrowed an old planter and planted potatoes. He anticipated making lots of money when the summer was over.

During the summer, it was necessary to weed. One-half acre is a lot of weeding with a hoe. We encouraged him. He had to hill the potatoes twice during the season. Hilling is pulling soil up around the vines so the potatoes don't grow out of the ground and turn green in the long, sunny days. It seemed like he spent the entire summer working in the potato field.

Finally, harvesttime arrived. Roger dug the potatoes with a borrowed potato digger. It didn't have a sacker, so the digger spilled the potatoes and the vines onto the ground. Then, it was time to pick them up and put them into sacks. Roger wore a potato-picking belt, a wide belt with several hooks attached. Some of the hooks are used for empty gunny sacks. Two of them are used to hold the sack open while potatoes are thrown between the feet and into the sack. This is done while bending over. At the end of the day Roger felt his back was permanently fused into a bending-over position. He finished picking up the potatoes in the rain on the second day.

He kept enough of his crop to last our family for the winter. This satisfied the fertilizer loan from Bob. He kept out enough potatoes to fill orders from school teachers and other people. This paid off the seed bill. He trucked the rest to Palmer and put them in storage at the Matanuska Maid Co-op.

That winter, Roger got a storage bill for $150. The crop was sold later in the year. When he received his check, it was for $12 more than the storage bill. He had worked all summer for $12.

This was a good lesson about business and farming. He didn't make much money, but we had plenty of potatoes to eat that winter.

Plump Stump Sisters

The "Women Who Stole the Show," the headline read. The Plump Stump Sisters were at it again!

The first time the Plump Stump Sisters performed was in the early 60s at a neighborhood Homemaker's Club Christmas party. The club asked each family to contribute a talent. Three friends, Marj, Mary, and Lois said, "Let's form a funny little group and play something." They decided Mary would play the washboard, Marj, the piano, and Lois, the accordion.

They dressed in genuine, homesteader-type clothes. Mary, topped with a floppy hat, wore a blue taffeta dress with high heels and anklets—Minnie Pearl style. Lois dressed the same way, only added an old fur coat collar, and draped it around her neck. She also had a stuffed poodle on a leash. When she jerked it, the dog flipped over. Marj wore dark sunglasses, a pill-box hat topped with flowers, high heels, and men's stockings. The three women looked like something out of Beverly Hillbillies!

When Johnnie's Bar in Wasilla had their grand opening, the Plump Stump Sisters played at the bar's fashion show and dinner. They played country-western music such as "Oh, Lonesome Me," "Daddy's Hands," "I'm My Own Grandpa," and others. They also played in Talkeetna, at the Willow Winter Carnival, and at the Moose Club in Palmer.

There was a great demand for them in Wasilla. After their Willow performance, the local newspaper headlined them as the "Women Who Stole the Show."

At the Talkeetna talent show, they spent the night with their husbands at the Fairview Inn and had the finest time, dancing all night. Rooms were $2 a night—the same price whether two or 10 shared the room.

Later that week, at an important basketball game at the local high school, Mary's husband, Red, used a bathroom plunger as a baton to direct the group. Lois wore white gloves. Finger by finger she elegantly took her gloves off before starting to play, and tossed them in the air. One landed against the rough-surfaced concrete block wall and stuck. Everyone laughed. The audience thought she'd done this on purpose, but it just happened.

Before they performed at the game, Lois was waiting outside the entrance of the school for the other two members of the group. A friend of hers approached saying, "I didn't recognize you, I thought you were a homesteader from Willow."

Later that winter, the Plump Stump Sisters were invited to the Moose Club in Anchorage to perform in another talent show. Red, being tall in stature, wore an outfit three sizes too small and too short. He wore red long johns under his 'too small' suit and again used a plunger as a baton.

Responding to an ad in the Palmer Frontiersman for people to take part in the local PTA talent show, the group decided to put on an act. The Plump Stump Sisters, their husbands, and Bob and I constructed a simple scene—an outhouse, a cabin, and props, and used them to show what homesteaders do to conceal illegal moose operations. Even though it was corny, it was well received.

The Plump Stump Sisters were also asked to participate in a fashion show at the Westward Hotel in Anchorage. It was a fancy affair, and the three of them sat around imitating each other and saying very haughtily and comically, "We're going to Anchorage and hobnob with those fancy rich people." Their performance was a big hit, and they got their picture on the front page of the Anchorage Times. They played at events for over two years. Mary said their act could have grown into something big. They had fun, even if it embarrassed their kids. The kids were worried about their mothers' reputations. Paula, Mary's pre-teen daughter, was the most embarrassed. To her, it was important to act and look decent.

Paula resented her mother being called plump. She thought she would never amount to anything because her mother paraded in public in old clothes and acted the fool. She wondered what kind of degenerate family she was coming from. She saw her mother with fake freckles, wearing old clothes, drumming on wood, and attempting a rendition of the Charleston.

Two years from the time the Plump Stump Sisters began their act, it became too much of a good thing and took away from their family time, so they disbanded. They missed being in the spotlight. It hadn't cost a dime and in those days people had to make their entertainment or become reclusive. The community was more closely knit back then when people had to draw on their inexpensive resources. I really miss the Plump Stump Sisters. No one can take those wonderful memories away from me.

Epilogue

We arrived in Alaska light on assets, young, vigorous, in good health, and optimistic about the future. Except for being young, this still applies to us today. Homesteading was exciting and full of experiences and each day was a new Alaska adventure. Life was hard, but we met each problem with determination and ambition. We learned that it isn't what happens to you, it's how you react that matters.

Our memories are of hard work, dreams, disappointments, plus many pleasant experiences. Many of our homestead friends are still around and unfortunately some have passed on to the big homestead in the sky. We are in the fall of our years, with the energy of spring chickens, and look forward to our next Alaska adventure.

www.ingramcontent.com/pod-product-compliance
Lightning Source LLC
Chambersburg PA
CBHW052043090426
42739CB00010B/2027